# Full Share

To Art

T. J. Smith

Sept 98

# Full Share

## Claiming Your Birthright to Energy, Growth, Love, and Fulfillment

**THEODORE J. SMITH, M.D., F.A.C.P.**

Whitewing Press
TUCSON

*Full Share*

Whitewing Press
Tucson, Arizona

Library of Congress Catalog Card No. 95-60225
ISBN 0-9639519-0-4



Designed and produced by Harrison Shaffer
Edited by Jeffrey H. Lockridge

∞ This book was printed on acid-free, archival quality paper.
Manufactured in the United States of America

# Contents

**Preface** **xi**

1. **Understanding Your Fears and Defenses** **1**
   - What Are You Afraid Of? 1
   - Learning, Knowledge, and Wisdom 2
   - Defenses Are Learned 3
   - Hang-Ups Are Defenses 4
   - Defenses Maintain the Status Quo 5
   - Awareness versus Fear 7
   - Defenses Are Unneeded 8
   - Your Belief System 9
   - Your Conscious Mind 10
   - Your Subconscious Mind—and How to Direct It 11
   - You Can Change 15
   - Summary 16

2. **Age-Dating Your Personality Arrests: The Smith Index** **19**
   - Born Six Years Too Soon 19
   - Spontaneous Age Reenactment 20
   - We All Pretend 22

The Smith Index: Before Birth to Five Years of Age 22
Infancy 23
Childhood 26
Summary 27

3. INFANCY: Before Birth to Two and a Half Years of Age 29
**Before Birth** **29**
**Birth to Age One** **30**
Violent Temper 30
Rage, Tantrums, and Vandalism 31
Juvenile Delinquency, Wife Beating, and Other Criminal Behavior 32
Child Beating 34
Irritability 35
Craving for Physical Contact: Smoking, Compulsive Sex 36
Shut-Off Feelings: Emotional Coldness 37
**Age One** **38**
The Spoiled Child 38
Overeating: Obesity 39
Sexual Inhibitions, Modesty, Poor Body Image 44
Stealing 46
Codependency 47
**Age Two to Two and a Half** **47**
Defiance 49
Selfishness 50
Evasiveness: Running Away 50
Profanity 51

Frigidity 52
Alcoholism and Other Self-Destructive Behavior 53
Summary 55

**4. CHILDHOOD: Two and a Half to Five Years of Age 57**
**Age Two and a Half to Three 57**
Aggressiveness and Passive Aggressiveness 58
Anxiety, Worry 59
Indecisiveness 60
Depression 61
Pretentiousness: Putting on Airs 61
**Age Three 62**
Blind Obedience 62
Fault 63
Guilt 64
Shame 65
Ridding Yourself of Fault, Guilt, and Shame 66
The Nice Person 67
The Perfectionist 68
The Con Artist 69
Fairness 69
Jealousy 70
Sarcasm, Bitterness and Resentment 71
**Age Four 72**
Lying 72
Suppressed Emotional Expression: Bed Wetting 74
Learning Disability: Stupidity as a Defense 74
Impotence 76
Laziness, Procrastination 76

Inappropriate Smile and Laughter 78
Stammering 79
**Age Five** **79**
Competitiveness 80
Criticism 80
Dogmatism 81
Bigotry, Hatred, and Vengefulness 82
The Dreamer: Fantasy versus Imagination 84
Summary 85

**5. Your Self-Image and How You Relate to Others** **87**
Choices 87
Truth 89
No Abnormal Behavior 90
Needs versus Wants 91
Worship 91
Love 93
Groups 94
Marriage 95
Divorce 99
Teenage Gangs 101
Teenage Pregnancy 103
Emotional Age and Sexual Expression 104
Use of Prostitutes, Casual Sex 107
Sexual Abuse of Children: Incest 108
Emotions and the Tree of Life 109
Summary 111

**6. Understanding Your Behavior** **113**
Two Views of Human Nature 113
Why—Our Blessing and Our Curse 114
Trusting Your Intuition 118
A Safe Place 119
Common Sense 121
Passage of Time 121
Alcohol, Drugs, and Self-Abuse 122
Security and the Generic Person 124
Self-Destructiveness, Suicide, and the Ending of Life 126
Intuition and the Acceptance of Reality 127
Ultimate Freedom: *Being* 128
Summary 129

**7. Parenting Yourself as You Parent Your Children** **131**
Trapped in Your Past 131
Emotional Growth 132
Changing the Pictures in Your Subconscious Mind 133
Reaching into Your Subconscious Mind 134
Honesty 136
Expectations 138
Basic Steps for Change 139
Guide for Parenting 140
- Accept and Love Your Children 141
- Set Reasonable, Impartial Limits 142
- Have Faith in Your Children 144
- Stick to the Affirmative 144

Talk to Your Children Eye to Eye 146
Teach Your Children by Example 148
Encourage and Support Your Children 149
Summary 151

**8. Techniques And Exercises** **153**
Control 153
Undoing Should, Ought, and Must 153
Relaxation: Flow versus Control 155
Centering 157
Relaxing, Reconditioning, Healing 158
Age-Dating Personality Arrests 163
Monitoring Your Defenses 165
Age Regression to Past Lives 166
Screen Door 167
A Cup of Coffee 167
Back from the Future 168
Cloning Yourself 170
Influencing Your Young Children 171
Your Dreams and Your Defenses 172
"Bad Dreams": Reprogramming Your Subconscious Mind 174
Summary 176

**Conclusion** **177**

**Appendix: Directed Age Reenactment** **179**

**Glossary** **185**

# Preface

After practicing as a specialist in internal medicine in a general medical clinic in Tacoma, Washington, for seventeen years, I realized I wasn't reaching the root cause of illness in a large proportion of my patients. It seemed clear to me that perhaps as many as fifty percent of my patients were reacting mainly to emotional conflicts rather than to any primary disease process. I was ameliorating their current physical symptoms, but I wasn't addressing the underlying emotional cause of their problems.

In order to understand the emotional conflicts that generated my patients' physical symptoms, and disenchanted with the narrow, cognitive approach of standard psychological and psychiatric models to patient symptoms and behavior, I undertook additional studies in hypnoanalysis. In this discipline the thrust is to discover and understand which past experiences conditioned patients to react to their present everyday life—to identify what actually happened to them in the past that causes them to react the way they do now, and when it happened.

I conducted thousands of directed age reenactments and amassed a wealth of primary data concerning the origins of personality arrests. After careful study of case histories, I became aware of common patterns that blocked natural emotional development during the first six years of a child's life. These patterns—emotional defenses or personality arrests—persisted and became reinforced over time, until they eventually trapped those who exhibited them at an infantile or childish level of emotional development.

Each defense, no matter how immaturely or inappropriately it was now expressed, could be traced back to a definite age and set of circumstances when it was both understandable and appropriate. By guiding my patients back to that age, by helping them reexperience and place those circumstances in the broadest perspective, I was able to start them on the path to releasing their defense and to resuming their emotional development.

I have made little or no attempt to correlate my findings with those of other investigators; rather, the material presented here reflects what I have learned from twenty-five years' experience working directly with patients.

## ACKNOWLEDGMENTS

I wish to thank my wife, Elizabeth Taft-Smith, for helping me develop and refine the principles of this book; my editor, Jeffrey H. Lockridge, for working hard to make the text more readable; my son, Kim York Smith, M.D., for his contributions to the sections on parenting; author Lorraine Owens for her comments and support; and Harrison Shaffer of Whitewing Press for guiding the book safely into print.

# 1

# Understanding Your Fears and Defenses

## WHAT ARE YOU AFRAID OF?

We come into the world with no fears or emotional defenses. We don't need them . . . yet. We are born mentally and emotionally equipped with the natural power and force to succeed in whatever we attempt. We have the potential to mature into fully developed, warm, open, and loving adults. We are born with the natural inclination to succeed. Our only deterrents to emotional maturity are our hang-ups—our **personality arrests**—the emotional defenses we learn in our first six years as we respond to perceived threats and to the fears and anger of our parents.

As a newborn infant, you feel everything in terms of life and death. You perceive danger as a threat to your very existence, and you perceive every threat, whether emotional or physical, in the same way. Rejection and anger on the part of your **parent** become for you fear of starvation, abandonment, or death; indeed, when you are very young and vulnerable, there are many forces and situations that can cause death in no time at all.

Suppose a few days after birth you are hungry. Your mother has you on a feeding schedule, but you lack that information. You cry because you are hungry now and haven't learned that soon you will be fed. You may fear you have been abandoned and will die unless someone comes immediately to feed you. You don't know or care who feeds you, as long as your need is satisfied. You learn that if you cry, someone will come in and care for you.

When, as an infant or child, you wake up in the night feeling cold and alone, you react as if you have been abandoned. You scream and thrash about until someone comes to relieve your plight—to reassure you that you haven't been abandoned and that your life is no longer threatened. You have learned how to save your life. When this happens repeatedly over a long time, it becomes a fixed reaction—an **emotional defense**.

How you react today when you are in fear, angry, or under stress will depend on your experiences and the defenses you learned during your first six years of life. As an adult, when you find yourself in a threatening situation, your subconscious mind will search for your earliest similar threat and will immediately activate the defense you learned then to avert the threat. Thus the threat you perceive in your *current* situation induces infantile or childish behavior—appropriate to your situation *then*, but no longer appropriate in your adult life. Nevertheless, you are still **behaving as** a fearful, angry infant or child in need of this defense. Because your reaction to the perceived threat occurs unconsciously, in milliseconds, you have no way at that moment to understand either your original situation or your initial reaction.

## LEARNING, KNOWLEDGE, AND WISDOM

You learn by acquiring information and by practicing ways to use it, but **knowledge** is inherited from generations of forebears. Your knowledge, like an ear for music or the talent for fine manipulation of the fingers, is your birthright.

You gain access to it through your creative imagination by tuning into the common consciousness. **Wisdom**, in turn, is the deeper understanding of the world acquired by combining **learning** with knowledge.

If this book makes sense to you, it is because you already *know* the ideas it conveys—you already have them in your mind. I am only providing a means for you to reexamine them. If you read on, you are simply allowing yourself to reconsider an approach you had formerly bypassed to look into your past experiences and to understand afresh how they have shaped your **self-image**. You will reject ideas that don't feel right for you, but those that do won't slip away from you again.

All of us pretend to be more adult than we feel and to strive for a higher place in the human order than we believe we are entitled to, but when external pressure becomes overwhelming, each of us **behaves as** a fearful, angry infant or child—emotionally returning to the time we first learned a particular defense. We change (grow) only by allowing our perceptions to shift as we gather more information about the event that resulted in our defense and integrate it to form a more complete picture.

## DEFENSES ARE LEARNED

Like every living organism from the smallest one-celled animal to a whale, when you feel you are being attacked, you defend yourself with the resources available to you. The next time you feel threatened in a similar way, you will use the old defense, reinforced by the new experience. Your body's immune system develops antibodies to microbes only after you are first sensitized to them. Your emotional defenses parallel that development, and your first exposure to a perceived threat is called the "**initial sensitizing event**."

Suppose you are a month old. Your mother has you on a four-hour feeding schedule and during the time between feedings she leaves to do chores or errands. Suppose also you are a baby who gets suddenly very hungry. Mother knows she will be back in time to feed you before you starve to death, but you, as a helpless infant, cannot feed yourself, you cannot fend for yourself if, as you fear, you are abandoned. You will have the same feeling of abandonment whether your mother returns in only a short time or whether she has left you to die on a rocky hillside or in a dark forest. From your infant's perspective, you feel she has abandoned you and that you need food and attention this minute or you will perish.

So, you scream and thrash about until you receive attention. When this happens, your conclusion is that your outbursts saved your life. You may be left alone repeatedly. Each time your panic becomes more intense. You express it by crying and thrashing about even more. When your mother returns, picks you up, strokes and feeds you, your conclusion —the defense you learn—will be that your crying and screaming made her return and thereby saved your life.

Once you react and successfully defend yourself, you have learned that defense for life. When you feel a similar threat of abandonment, you will use the same defense again and again. Emotionally, you **behave as** you did when you first learned the defense in your infancy.

As an infant, you act first for self-preservation and survival—like any other baby animal. As you grow older, you may be able to delay your first impulses and choose a more mature response. The intensity of your emotional defenses will depend entirely on when you first perceived a threat. The closer to birth you first felt threatened, the more vulnerable you were—and the more urgent your need to defend yourself. And the more urgent your need was *then*, the more intense your defense will be in later life.

## HANG-UPS ARE DEFENSES

We all develop our own. There are two types of hang-ups. The first is related directly to physical survival. The second, which is more complicated, relates to our individual need to establish an identity and to fulfill our potential by developing our talents. Defenses related to physical survival are the dominant type. Many times we will sacrifice our individuality in order not to risk rejection, for in the infant mind of our defenses, rejection is tantamount to death.

Fear and defenses are intricately related. A defense is created as a result of a fear. The basic nature of **fear** is imagination; fear blocks any logic or consideration of reason. If you, as a small child, felt rejected, your fear and resulting defense are going to protect you from that feeling—no matter what. Even if in reality there is little chance as an adult you would be rejected in a similar situation, you repeatedly **behave as** you learned in early childhood. Logic does not prevail—defense takes over. What you feel is your reality. Fear of heights, of confined spaces, or even of aggressive persons can be traced all the way back to a picture first recorded in early infancy or childhood.

Your defenses always keep you one step removed from the danger that gave rise to them. If you are hurt, say, in a fall from a high ledge, you develop the fear of being injured in the same way. Consequently, you keep yourself from falling again by never consciously allowing yourself to be on a high, unprotected place.

## DEFENSES MAINTAIN THE STATUS QUO

If you have a fear of heights, the fact that you can easily walk mile after mile on a twelve-inch wide path through a flat, grassy meadow will in no way help you walk a twelve-inch beam ten feet up in the air. The subject is closed, even to abstract discussion. My attempting to force you to walk the beam will serve only to reinforce your fear. Nor can you expect to mature spontaneously in that area. Such is the nature of hang-ups. Only if you allow yourself to become aware of and to accept the initial sensitizing event behind your hang-up, and only if you then acquire additional information about it, will you be able to shift your perception and release your fear.

More than anything else, defenses work to maintain the status quo. One of the most insidious forms of defense occurs at times in your life when you feel fulfilled, confident, and on top of the world. Suddenly, everything seems to go wrong. Depression and feelings of unworthiness start to creep in. "Why is it when I'm on top of the world, I'm not happy?" The answer is that, deep down inside, you feel you don't deserve it.

This is a classic example of a defense mechanism at work. When everything is riding high and you suddenly experience a drop in spirits, there is a saboteur at work—yourself. If you had an unstable environment during your early years, you may feel the safest place now is an environment similar to the one you experienced in your childhood, when you were at a disadvantage. No matter how bad it was, it feels safer compared to an unknown environment. You know how to deal with your "betters," even if it displeases your conscious mind. You re-create the havoc in your life so that you can again reside in the *known* environment of your past. To a varying degree, you suffer from a self-image problem and may actually destroy whatever is very dear to you—a marriage, a friendship, a career—because you don't feel you deserve to be in such a good situation. You are uncomfortable with the praise or compliments accorded you, hence you proceed to behave in a way that will relieve your discomfort.

Suppose that, when you were two or three years old, someone very important to you—your older brother, for example—was highly insecure in his own identity. Furthermore, suppose your brother got his sense of worth by being first and best at everything he did. As an alert, responsive child, you tried everything to please him. But no matter what you did, your brother criticized your performance or ordered you to do it again "the right way." The only performance that didn't threaten this insecure person was one in which you remained inept and uncompetitive, and thus maintained the status quo. Throughout your life, every time you reach a high point of accomplishment, your performance creates insecurity within you, and your defense again requires you to become inept and dependent—to maintain the status quo.

How can you escape your own learned traps? The key to real growth is to revise the pictures in your memory bank and the conclusions you carry within your subconscious mind. You have the power to change everything about your emotional life that causes you hurt. Your defenses operate on beliefs formed with only partial information concerning the initial sensitizing event. You will change your defenses only when you allow change in your basic belief system. And you will change your belief system only when you voluntarily accept and expand reality by accommodating additional information to augment the images now implanted in your mind.

Because your reaction is involuntary, the prime requisite to effect change is to have a safe place. Even a slight confrontation will evoke your defenses. A therapist must be completely nonjudgmental in order to provide a safe place; in group therapy, all members must be completely accepting before you will feel safe enough to expose your emotional self.

You must first understand, not *why* you now respond as you do, but *where* your defenses originated. *Why* demands logic, and emotional defenses are the antithesis of logic, except when you had your first sensitizing experience; then and *only* then was your response to emotions logical.

## AWARENESS VERSUS FEAR

The opposite to fear is **awareness** and understanding. When you are fully aware of a situation, when you understand it completely, you will take the necessary action to put yourself in a more favorable position. Fear blocks your awareness, interferes with your understanding, and thus greatly impairs your effectiveness to act.

Emotional hang-ups are fear that results in defenses. No one needs them. Fear is almost always an imagined danger that gets in the way of the most expeditious means you may take to avoid harm to your person or individuality. If you walk dark city streets frequented by drug dealers, muggers, and robbers, you know there is a high probability you will be assaulted. Being fearful does you no practical good. What you really need is awareness, not fear. Fear constricts the thought process and blocks awareness of your immediate surroundings.

A split-second defense reaction is vital in averting sudden dangers. But for prolonged and emotional situations, bodily reactions as a defense are useless; they serve to isolate you from being in contact with your environment. Because they isolate you, defenses prevent you from experiencing life as it is. Like a castle or a fort, it may seem that you are safe inside, but the world and nature are all *outside* these self-imposed walls. The very thing that will make you stronger—emotional growth—will occur only when you *shed* your defenses. Defenses constrict your behavior, your personality, and thus your ability to deal with life.

## DEFENSES ARE UNNEEDED

An evolved person needs no defenses. To be fully alive and aware, you need to shed all your defenses. When you have a complete and total awareness of every sight, sound, smell, and intuitive feeling and are in touch with the information in your subconscious mind, then life's decisions are exceedingly easy to make. It is when you make decisions in confusion, with *partial* information, that you find yourself in difficulty.

Whenever you defend yourself by justifying or rationalizing your present attitude or present position, you automatically exclude emotional growth. Change isn't possible when you are on the defensive, whether consciously or unconsciously—and without some change, nothing can ever get better.

## YOUR BELIEF SYSTEM

How many times have you asked yourself, "If only I could do what's good for me—if only I could quit smoking, stop being so angry all the time, lose weight"?

You can't always do what is good for you because a deeper part of you sees all this "good for me" stuff as a con job. The problem is that you are pitting your logical, **conscious mind** against your **subconscious mind**, which protects you from change. You may tell yourself one thing, but because of what you have experienced in the past, you may feel something else. Trying to control your emotions or your environment for any length of time is an exercise in futility; your conscious mind through your voluntary actions cannot hope to overcome and dominate your subconscious mind and defense system.

To understand how this is so, you need to understand how your mind works. It is useful to divide the mind into two distinct, yet interacting parts: the **conscious mind**—what you *think* or *want* yourself to be; and the **subconscious mind**—what you *know* or *feel* yourself to be.

Corresponding to this division are the concepts of **self-portrait** and **self-image**. **Self-portrait** is your *conscious* picture of yourself (what you *want* to be), which governs the way you act when your life is relatively unchallenged—and which (until challenged) you pretend is your true self. By contrast, **self-image** is your *subconscious* image of yourself (what you *feel* you are), which ultimately directs or limits all your behavior.

An impressive self-portrait is especially helpful in today's society, where even a person of modest ability in music, art, politics, or life itself can, through self-promotion, achieve considerable success. On the other hand, it is not unusual for a celebrity with a great self-portrait and immense popularity to have a low self-image. When under duress or emotional stress, the celebrity may even self-destruct in alcohol or drugs, or reckless behavior, or rage, **behaving as** the fearful infant or child of his or her self-image.

## YOUR CONSCIOUS MIND

Many of us assume that the conscious mind is stronger and more complex than the subconscious mind, but how many thoughts can you carry on in your head at once without getting them confused or forgetting something? One, two, possibly three? If you are brilliant, you may be able to switch rapidly from one thought to the other and keep a number of thoughts going on at one time, but you are soon likely to tire or get distracted.

In spite of our advanced evolution, we have very limited conscious capacity to control bodily processes and defenses—or even to form new ideas. Your conscious intellect can only *confirm* what you or others already know. Creativity is all *sub*conscious. Your conscious mind-set is that if you haven't done something that way before, you cannot do it now. Your conscious mind can and does make judgments, apply logic, compare ideas to see which idea is most practical, achievable, or cost-effective. But mulling over any idea with your conscious mind alone will tell you nothing new or different. Indeed, rehashing and eliminating choices may lead your conscious mind to the conclusion that *nothing* is possible.

Your conscious mind is like an editor who organizes someone else's ideas, rejecting those that don't go together or won't appeal to his readers, judging whether a particular idea might work, but not coming up with any ideas of his own. Ideas come from the subconscious mind. Judgments *about* ideas come from the conscious mind.

You can consciously will the muscles of your hand to move, but even the least of these movements requires coordination with your subconscious mind to hold the remainder of your body in an "at ease" position while you move, say, the little finger of one hand. (Meanwhile, the subconscious is regulating your blood pressure, the muscle tone of your arms, legs, and torso, and a myriad other bodily processes.) We like to think we (our *conscious* minds) are in control of ourselves, but we cannot consciously control the over ninety percent of us that is under the jurisdiction of the subconscious mind.

You can imagine a beautifully cooked roast and you may actually salivate, but you cannot order your saliva to flow. You can picture a romantic scene with your lover and you may become sexually aroused, but you cannot order yourself to respond. And you can read a horror story and you may become terribly frightened, but you cannot order your heart to pump faster or your skin to produce goose bumps.

## YOUR SUBCONSCIOUS MIND —AND HOW TO DIRECT IT

Your subconscious mind has thousands of clear channels that can operate independently or in concert with each other and that regulate at least ninety percent of your bodily processes automatically. Your subconscious mind can make the pupils of your eyes dilate, your throat constrict, your small intestine digest, and your toes sweat all at once, separately, or in any combination. Every day it controls these and thousands of other bodily processes. (Your conscious mind, on the other hand, can directly control only your skeletal muscles.) Indeed, your total coordination, your bodily defenses, and your well-being are all managed by your subconscious mind.

Although you cannot control, you can *direct* your subconscious mind. Which is what this book is about—learning how to direct your emotional energy favorably. You can do this, as the examples at the end of the previous section suggest, through active imagery—by *consciously* imagining in vivid detail. Although there is no simple, direct method to release fear and overcome hang-ups, by repeating the following steps (described at length in the chapters to come), you can over time change your feelings about a perceived threat and thus change your reactions and behavior in the face of it.

First, *identify* the unwanted behavior or emotional defense, say, procrastination: you always put off starting a project, even though you know it has to be done—and even though you may *like* to do it. Second, *age-date* your defense on the Smith Index—procrastination is typically a four-year-old personality arrest. Then, with the help of a therapist trained in **directed age reenactment**, do the following. Third, *think back* to when you were four years old. Remember what happened then. Look for the time you first felt afraid to try anything, for when you were first told, "You don't know how to do that!" or "You can't do that!" or "You're doing that wrong!" Fourth, *visualize* in vivid detail the circumstances that first led you to learn your defense—the initial sensitizing event; fifth, *reenact* this event, reexperiencing all the emotions you felt then, and bringing to bear all the information you have accumulated in the past ten to fifty or more years; and sixth, in the light of this information, *recognize* that, however much you needed your defense then, you *no longer* need it.

You can also direct your subconscious mind by *suspending* your imagination—by putting your imagery in neutral. Through such techniques as meditation, yoga, and biofeedback, you can temporarily suspend your internal images and dialogues of worry, fear, and anxiety, giving yourself a respite, and even loosening up some of your emotional defenses or blocks. But until you uncover and release the fears behind your anxious images and the defenses that have created them, techniques directed at behavior change (such as hypnosis to quit smoking, lose weight, and so forth) are likely to have only short-term success—and to *reinforce* your defenses in the long term.

Your subconscious mind has four highly integrated functions. The first, most primitive function (also present in all the so-called lower animals) is to control your autonomic nervous system, which manages at least ninety percent of your bodily processes automatically, including your five physical senses (sight, touch, taste, smell, and hearing), your immune system, and all your physical reflexes.

The second function is to store memories of everything you have experienced or thought. Your subconscious memory is virtually unlimited: each bit of information is filed and cross-indexed as a distinct **image** in an almost endless number of ways. Experiences with high emotional content form your most prominent, most accessible memories—those that need to be readily available for your defense system. Experiences with low emotional content are only lightly etched in your memory and are therefore almost inaccessible, unless etched more deeply by many repetitions. Like real life, your memory records contain all of the sensory components of the original experiences. These take the form of images with elements from some or all of your six senses—sight, touch, taste, smell, hearing, and **intuition** (commonly called the "sixth sense").

The third function of your subconscious mind is to activate your emotional defenses and reactions. Your subconscious first compares templates formed from memory images of past experiences with images from current experiences—whether actual, imagined, or dreamed. When it finds a match, or near-match, using the selected template's memory images, it then activates the autonomic nervous system and, in turn, the bodily reactions we interpret as emotions, as well as any defenses that go with the images.

The fourth function of your subconscious mind is intuitive and creative thought—spontaneous thinking in whole concepts or images, which comes to the fore only when your conscious mind relinquishes control. You have always directed your subconscious mind, although you have probably been unaware of it. You do so constantly by a kind of self-hypnosis, by the images and pictures you conjure up from minute to minute. Some of these you form *consciously* by combining or rearranging other images, some come in dreams, but the bulk come from memories. For every learned experience, you have a picture you replay and a corresponding set of habitual bodily reactions controlled by your subconscious mind, such as those for preparing to go to bed, opening the refrigerator and taking out the milk, driving your car, and even walking downstairs. By consciously calling forth certain pictures held in your subconscious mind, you can also call forth the reactions directed by those pictures. Accurate or not, the pictures stored in your subconscious mind constitute your personal truth. But included among your learned experiences are your defenses and hang-ups. These are triggered *un*consciously, when external circumstances act directly upon your subconscious, calling forth pictures and corresponding reactions most often inappropriate to your current situation. The only way to change your defense reactions is to change the pictures that evoke those reactions and that you believe are real.

It is difficult for you to overcome your hang-ups because you have replayed them so many thousands of times over the years, and the more you have replayed them, the more deeply these hang-ups have become entrenched. Suppose, for example, when you were two years old, every time you cried, made noise, or asked your mother for something, she said, "Shut up or I'll kill you," or "If you cry or bother me once more, you're going to get it." As a two-year-old, you didn't understand that your mother was using a figure of speech when she threatened you. You believed you had to be quiet or you would be killed or severely beaten.

Years later, at school, you speak out once or twice and receive disapproving glances from a teacher or a classmate. Instantly, the threat of death or severe beating plays across your subconscious mind, and you are too frightened to say anything else. The class ends, you walk out unharmed—protected by this defense learned as an infant—and the defense is again reinforced. Once more, you get by the best way you know—you clam up.

Time and time again, you cling to this defense because unconsciously you feel you will die without it, even though what you learned as a child may have nothing to do with your adult life, and even though no one would have hurt you, let alone killed you, for speaking your opinion. Warranted or not, your fear *feels* very real. The pictures implanted in your mind during your early childhood are replayed over and over; each time the defense "works" for you, it becomes more entrenched.

## YOU CAN CHANGE

When we are threatened, we respond in much the same way each and every time we are exposed to circumstances that suggest a past experience to our subconscious minds. Take your father, mother, or an old friend, for example. Over the years, they have mellowed (blocked their reactions) but, if you probe a little deeper, you will find that their reactions have not changed in twenty years. Their attitude about your worth or ability, or their fear of other races, say, has changed little in the past two decades.

We all have hang-ups—emotional defenses that we can't eliminate simply by programming our conscious minds with a few happy sayings, affirmations, or New Year's resolutions. These defenses have been implanted—originally for self-preservation—in your subconscious mind. You must work with the information stored at that deep subconscious level. Change comes only as you add and accept new information about the circumstances of your original experiences.

Although you cannot change your past environment, your mother, your father, your friends, your children, your spouse, or even yourself (directly), you *can* change your perceptions and consequently your expectations—your self-image. But to upgrade your self-image, you must allow yourself to gather and appraise added information. All your conclusions are based on what you have learned—on information you have collected in the past. As you learn more and become more aware, you no longer will hold your old "truth" to be inviolable.

A closed mind blocks your chances for growth and brings stagnation, senility, and death, both intellectual and emotional. But an open mind lets you learn more—acquire added information—and thus enlarge your former awareness and adjust your conclusions, which, in turn, will change your perceptions and your expectations.

Rest assured, this task is by no means superhuman. Your defenses are the consequence of normal emotions. This book offers you a simple, effective approach to understanding your emotions; in the chapters that follow you will learn how, on your own and with the help of a therapist trained in directed age reenactment, you can

- *identify* and *age-date* your defenses;
- *consciously return* to the initial sensitizing events behind your defenses;
- *change* through additional information the pictures implanted in your subconscious;
- *reexperience* the feelings associated with these pictures;
- *release* the fears and anger behind your defenses—and thus the defenses themselves; and in so doing,
- *unblock* your emotional growth.

My hope and principal aim in writing this book is that, as you learn to free yourself from the fears and anger blocking your emotional growth, you will help your children free themselves from their fears and anger as well, allowing each of you to reach your fullest potential.

## SUMMARY

**Fear** is the main self-limiting factor in your life. You create some of your fear, but you learn most from your parents. As an infant or child, you respond to fear and **anger** by forming **emotional defenses** to save yourself from rejection, abandonment, and death. Reinforced again and again as you grow older, these **personality arrests** or hang-ups can remain with you throughout your life, limiting your emotional growth.

Your **subconscious mind** manages ninety percent of your bodily processes, while your **conscious mind** controls only your voluntary (skeletal) muscles; even these have to be coordinated by your subconscious mind, which also manages your senses and **self-image**, as well as your fears, emotions, and emotional defenses.

Although you cannot control your subconscious mind, you can *direct* it. By visualizing in vivid detail the circumstances that first led you to form a particular emotional defense—the **initial sensitizing event**—by understanding those circumstances in their broadest terms, and by reexperiencing the emotions you then felt, you can release your fear or anger and overcome your defense. You can bring the sum total of your experience and **learning** as an adult to bear on the situation you faced as an infant or child. This book is dedicated to helping you understand and direct your subconscious mind to achieve self-acceptance, emotional maturity, and the fulfillment of your potential.

# 2

# Age-Dating Your Personality Arrests

## THE SMITH INDEX

### BORN SIX YEARS TOO SOON

As humans, we are born six years before we could possibly survive on our own. During those first six years, our parents mostly do a good job of protecting us physically to ensure our survival. That's the easy part. The hard part is providing us a safe place to develop emotionally—and especially not inflicting on us their own fears and anger, which in turn will cause personality arrests. More than any other animal, we learn during our first six years by what our parents tell us and what they do. As children, we soak up the habits and assume the hang-ups of our parents as surely as we learn to speak their language and dialect.

Emotional development has a definite progressive pattern and, like the embryo developing in the womb, we cannot go hopscotching through it. Missing or delaying one step in our emotional development will produce a void that can prevent normal development from that point on.

With the proper technique, you will have no difficulty in learning when you experienced a specific personality arrest.

This in turn will allow you to explore the circumstances surrounding the personality arrest and, like picking up a missed stitch in knitting and bringing the loops and the repair forward, to fill in the missing information when you become aware of what happened.

To understand people, you need to see them as they really are. This means accepting their actions without trying to explain or excuse them. Those actions were perfectly logical and reasonable at the initial sensitizing event—but *only* then; any attempt to logically explain them now will block you from understanding their situation as it exists today.

**Behave as** is the most important phrase you can adopt in understanding human emotions. When under stress, you **behave as** you were the moment you stopped growing emotionally. You spontaneously and automatically *reenact* the original feeling you had at that time. You **behave as** you were—and your defenses are those you had—at that moment, at that age. This is now your self-image; it reflects your basic belief system through your subconscious mind and your nervous system, and it will express itself in spite of all your attempts to suppress it.

## SPONTANEOUS AGE REENACTMENT

When people are under little or no stress, they can *seem* to be adults or whatever they consciously want to be. They can pretend to act differently from what they feel, but if you are an astute, objective observer, you will know what they are really feeling—from the nuances of their actions. These nuances will reflect their personality arrests and, provided you make no excuses or explanations about the provoking circumstances, will tell you at what age in infancy or childhood these arrests occurred.

When your actions aren't appropriate for a given situation, when they don't serve your best interests, then those actions don't belong to the here and now. You are *reenacting* them from another time and place, a much earlier time, when they *were* appropriate. This is called "**spontaneous age reenactment**"—or reliving part of your past.

When a college professor flares up in anger because his name is mispronounced, he is reacting—*reenacting* himself—as a two-year-old. A true adult would have no such reaction. Make no excuses about extenuating circumstances, make no allowances or rationalizations for this individual. If the professor **behaves as** a two-year-old, then emotionally that part of him *is* a two-year-old.

Like all living creatures, we are designed to fulfill our potential. We continue in that direction until some event blocks us emotionally. Logically, we could go *around* this blockage and continue toward our fulfillment, but instead, we learn a defense that will keep us from getting near that life-threatening situation a second time. The defense acts as a barrier so that part of us no longer explores or develops, and thus remains an unexplored and undeveloped potential and talent.

It is important to mention here that there are degrees of hang-ups. In general, the earlier you learn a defense, the more intense your struggle to survive and to defend yourself—and the stronger and more extensive your hang-up will be. If a basic drive is completely blocked or diverted, the defense or hang-up will be the most extensive. If the basic drive is only partially blocked, the hang-up will be harder to evoke and, once activated, will only be weakly or partially expressed.

These blocks and the defenses that go with them readily identify the specific age in our emotional development at which they were formed. Each of us comes with multiple ages. Most obvious is our chronological age. Next there is our mental age, and then our sexual development age. Finally there are our emotional ages—we have not one, but many, each different for a different type of feeling or situation. True fulfillment comes when we let ourselves mature in all these areas. Few of us have our act together.

## WE ALL PRETEND

All of us pretend when it comes to emotional age. We act the role we want ourselves to be, as though we were painting our own self-portrait: the loving parent, the wise leader, the competent professional, the efficient administrator. We can keep this charade up as long as we are not stressed or threatened. Under stress, all pretense falls away and we react at the level of our primitive defenses. This level will be at the age we first learned to defend ourselves for the sake of survival. This reaction causes us to **behave as** a threatened child, to *reenact* a sensitizing event that occurred during the first six years of life. You might become uncontrollably angry, jealous, fearful, you might blame everyone else or lie—you might react in any or all of these infantile or childish ways, depending on when that part of your personality was arrested—the specific age of your personality arrest.

Certain defenses are characteristic of definite stages—or ages—of development. The defenses are the same for all of us as developing humans.

## THE SMITH INDEX: BEFORE BIRTH TO SIX YEARS OF AGE

To reflect the major change that occurs in our emotional development around the age of two and a half, the Smith Index is divided into two parts. The first is **infancy**, which extends from before birth to about the age of two and a half. During this time, you are establishing your individuality single-handedly; because infants can't see the need for change, personality arrests formed in your infancy are more deeply rooted and usually harder to overcome. The second is **childhood**, which comprises the ages of two and a half to six. During this period, you are establishing and adjusting to your life as a member of the group; because children are more open to change than infants, personality arrests formed during your childhood are usually easier to overcome. By the age of six, your personality or self-image is all but fully formed.

The division reflects the change in your basic needs as a developing child. In infancy, your all-pervasive need is to be *accepted* as an individual. Without being recognized as an equal human being, an infant cannot develop normal emotions.

In childhood, ages two and a half to six, your basic need shifts from **acceptance** for *being* an individual to *approval* for *doing* and becoming a full member of your group. When you examine the entries on the Smith Index (pages 24–25), you will see that those in the first section (INFANCY) have as a common denominator the *need to be*, to be accepted, while those in the second (CHILDHOOD) have as a common denominator the *need to do*, to be approved.

## Infancy

**UNBORN: Sense Surroundings.** Through touch, hearing, and sight, you receive an ever-increasing amount of stimuli; as you develop in your mother's womb, you react to these stimuli in more and more refined ways.

**NEWBORN: Make Presence Known.** Still powerless to get what you want or avoid what you don't, you make your presence known by thrashing about and screaming to have someone satisfy your urgent needs.

**ONE-YEAR-OLD: Observe and Explore Surroundings.** You watch everything and everyone around you. You move to play with whatever attracts you within your arms' length—to touch it, grasp, squeeze, and smell it, pick it up, put it in your mouth, your ears, your nose—and you claim it as your own. The glass you break or the food you spill is of no importance to you, all you want is immediate fulfillment of your wishes even though you can't clearly express them.

## Smith Index—Age-Dating Personality Arrests

| INFANCY | |
|---|---|
| **Before Birth** | Claustrophobia<br>Schizophrenia |
| **Birth to One** | Craving for Physical Contact: Smoking, Compulsive Sex<br>Impatience<br>Shut-Off Feelings<br>Emotional Coldness<br>Irritability<br>Sense of Worthlessness<br>Violent Temper: Rage, Tantrums, Vandalism<br>Juvenile Delinquency<br>Wife, Child Beating<br>Other Criminal Behavior |
| **One to Two** | Spoiled Child<br>Overeating<br>Obesity<br>Sexual Inhibitions<br>Modesty<br>Poor Body Image<br>Sense of Helplessness<br>Codependency<br>Stealing |
| **Two to Two and a Half** | Fear of Intimacy<br>Profanity<br>Selfishness<br>Evasiveness<br>Running Away<br>Defiance<br>Frigidity<br>Sense of Unworthiness<br>Alcoholism<br>Self-Destructive Behavior |

## CHILDHOOD

| | |
|---|---|
| **Two and a Half to Three** | Pretentiousness, Putting on Airs; Anxiety, Worry; Indecisiveness; Depression (recurrent); Aggressiveness, Passive Aggressiveness |
| **Three to Four** | Fairness; Nice Person; Con Artist; Possessiveness, Jealousy; Perfectionist, Kleptomania, Anorexia Nervosa; Fault, Guilt, Shame; Sarcasm, Bitterness and Resentment; Blind Obedience |
| **Four to Five** | Inappropriate Smile and Laughter; Stammering; Bed Wetting; Learning Disability; Lying, Excuses; Laziness, Procrastination; Impotence |
| **Five to Six** | Dreamer: Fantasy vs. Imagination; Criticism; Argumentativeness; Competitiveness; Dogmatism; Bigotry, Hatred, Vengefulness |

**TWO- TO TWO-AND-A-HALF-YEAR-OLD: Establish Separate Identity.** You have learned to say NO! and can run away from harm or displeasure. You aren't concerned about pleasing others but are, instead, entirely focused on establishing your separate identity.

## Childhood

**TWO-AND-A-HALF- TO THREE-YEAR-OLD: Test Limits.** You have partly established your identity, but it remains fragile, in need of your parents' acceptance and support. You hold on to your toys and possessions; you aren't ready to share or cooperate. You are constantly testing the system to see how far you can go, but your energies can be diverted and channeled.

**THREE-YEAR-OLD: Seek to Participate.** You are clearly aware of your identity, and your feeling of self-importance is at an all-time high, but you begin to realize others also have identities and are important to you. They are not just Mother, Father, Sister, Brother—they are *your* father, *your* mother, *your* sister, *your* brother. At three, you want to be part of everything your family (or group) does.

**FOUR-YEAR-OLD: Seek Approval for Actions.** You are at your lifelong peak of needing to please others. You come to feel your existence depends on those around you, you are aware of their feelings, and you can now adjust your actions to accommodate others. You want others to approve of what you do, and you learn ways to get their approval. You are developing a sense of responsibility toward others, and you want to help.

**FIVE-YEAR-OLD: Learn Rules and How to Use Them.** In your sixth year of life, you learn how things are done and how to use the rules to achieve your ends. You are developing a sense of humor and are able to argue and shift positions; you form conclusions about your world and how it should be.

By six you have learned over half of everything you will ever know. Your creative thinking process has reached its peak, even though your ability to express that process continues to develop as you grow older. If your first six years of life are free from serious personality arrests, you maintain the exuberance and imagination of early childhood throughout your life, although, as a responsible adult, you can temporarily hold in check your expression of emotions and beliefs when you sense they might adversely affect the rights or sensitivities of others. From the age of six on, you will mostly accumulate and process information. Your basic emotional reactions and defenses have already solidly formed your self-image, which will shift little in the next ninety years. You have learned and practiced a complete set of human interpersonal emotional reactions. From now on, you will use combinations of defenses and refine and reinforce what you have already learned and practiced.

Unfortunately, because the greatest threat to any human being is other human beings, most of your defenses will be provoked by and directed toward other people. How you deal with life and other people in later years will only be a repetition and reinforcement of these six years of basic training; by and large, the greatest factor in your training has been what your parents said and did.

## SUMMARY

From before birth up to the age of six, a child's emotional development should be smooth and continuous. If, as an infant or child, you perceive that your survival is threatened, you will form an **emotional defense**. The severity of that defense—and of the arrest of that part of your personality—is in direct proportion to the severity of the threat. The earlier the threat, the more severely you are likely to perceive it—and the more severe your defense and your **personality arrest** are likely to be.

Later in life, when you encounter circumstances that remind your subconscious of the threat, you *spontaneously reenact* the time in **infancy** or **childhood** you first learned your defense. You **behave as** the frightened or angry infant or child you were then—even though the defense is *no longer* necessary.

To understand people, you must learn to see their behavior as it really is. **Behave as** is the most important phrase you can adopt in understanding human emotions. Different behaviors—reflecting different personality arrests—can be recognized as belonging to specific emotional ages, as shown in the Smith Index. Each emotional age has recognizable characteristics that can readily identify the emotional age of a particular personality arrest.

# 3

# INFANCY

## Before Birth to Two and a Half Years of Age

### BEFORE BIRTH

Over the nine months you are growing in your mother's womb, you develop an ever-increasing ability to receive and record sensory stimuli. You react to everything you can see, hear, and feel (physically and emotionally) around you—heartbeats, gurglings, and warmth from inside your mother's body; filtered light and muffled sounds from outside. You move, turn, and later kick.

You get all the oxygen and nourishment you need from your mother through the placenta; you are completely cared for and protected—so long as everything is well with Mother. When Mother is tense, angry, or frightened, you are totally immersed in her emotion. If Mother unsuccessfully attempts suicide or abortion, the threatening message gets through—but, as a fetus, you cannot run, strike out, or scream. Your only defense is to withdraw within yourself.

The defense you learned as an unborn infant may lead you later in life, when you feel threatened by circumstances that remind your subconscious of what you faced in the womb, either to withdraw into yourself (in extreme cases, **schizophrenia**) or to urgently seek escape from confinement (in severe cases, **claustrophobia**).

## BIRTH TO AGE ONE

You have, encoded in your genes, everything you need to overcome the trauma of birth, to survive the intense squeezing of your body and molding of your head as you are pushed through the birth canal, to survive the extreme transition from darkness, warmth, and liquid to bright light, cold, and air, and the even more extreme separation from your mother's body. You clear your lungs, breathe your first breath, and cry out.

In your first year of life in the outside world, you absorb and react, physically and emotionally, to a welter of sights, sounds, smells, tastes, and sensations. Your ability to act and to control your body, severely limited as a newborn, develops rapidly from six months on. You learn to sit and stand on your own, to grasp and hold objects, to crawl, to take your first steps, and finally to walk on your own. Throughout this time, your conscious mind, with its logic, reason, and critical discernment, is only beginning to develop; your activities and responses are governed almost entirely by your subconscious mind.

### VIOLENT TEMPER

**Anger** is one of our most primitive drives—present in all vertebrate animals. Designed to keep newborns alive at the instant they perceive a threat, explosive anger or rage, used repeatedly by infants before the age of one to protect themselves from their fear of rejection, abandonment, or death, becomes the emotional defense of violent temper. Violent temper in an older child or adult who feels threatened by other people or situations can control others through fright and intimidation, although it usually causes others to withdraw into themselves or get away from the violently angry or enraged person.

When you are being manipulated by a raging adult, you are in essence being cowed by a newborn infant out of control. To reason or argue with that adult makes no more sense than to reason or argue with an infant. The *newborn* emotional defense of violent temper is commonly accepted in our society as "normal" adult behavior.

## Rage, Tantrums, and Vandalism

As a newborn and during the first year of your life, you had very limited ways to communicate. If crying didn't attract the attention you needed, then around the age of two months you added thrashing about in rage. As a small, vulnerable baby, you felt you would die if you didn't get attention on the spot. This display of rage by tensing up, screaming, and turning blue is an entirely normal response—for a two-month-old baby. When, as a full-grown adult, you react to a situation by throwing a tantrum, you are *reenacting* a scene and a defense from your early infancy—no matter how grown-up you appear to be physically, you are **behaving as** a *newborn before the age of one*.

Only at one stage in our development, around three months old, when we have to lie on our backs because we can't yet roll over, stand up, or talk, do we resort to tantrums—kicking our feet, crying, having unintelligible outbursts of one kind or another. We feel helpless and frustrated, and we can't make ourselves understood in any other way. Older children or adults who have tantrums are reacting out of frustration and a feeling of powerlessness.

During adolescence, these tantrums may be acted out as vandalism. The vandal is **behaving as** a normal *three-month-old infant* with total disregard for others (except now, as a teenager, the vandal is strong and physically coordinated). It is highly likely the vandal had a crisis in his life when he was three months old that caused part of his personality to arrest at that stage of his emotional development. Today, he reverts to this behavior when he feels frustrated and totally powerless.

Because the newborn has such urgent need to be accepted and nurtured, this very early period is the only time in which a child spontaneously and normally becomes angry enough to kill. Even though, later in normal development, you learn that you don't die if you are left alone, you don't know that when you are an infant. As an adult, your perception is that your violent anger is actually saving your life, just as it did back when you were an infant. Once learned and practiced, this tried and true defense of violent temper will be evoked each time you feel truly threatened. At that moment you *are* the angry infant, with no thought of consequences.

Even though anger is a basic drive and cannot be eliminated from your feelings, you can do much to prevent the formation of the emotional defense of violent temper in your infant children. As you work with them, you will be able to tune into their needs *before* their anger progresses to rage. Pay attention to them; treat them with respect and as equals.

## Juvenile Delinquency, Wife Beating, and Other Criminal Behavior

The most important of all feelings, especially to an infant or child, is the feeling of acceptance. You are born into the world *expecting* to be accepted. If at or shortly after birth you feel rejected, the results can be devastating to the formation of your self-image.

Even as a newborn infant, you will seek an answer to the question "*Why* am I rejected?" The information you have is very limited; therefore, it is very possible that you will conclude: "My parents don't want me," "There must be something wrong with me," "I must be no good."

When you feel rejection, you try desperately to explain *why* your parents won't touch you, *why* they won't love or accept you. As you grow older, your attitude becomes

"Whatever I do doesn't matter to them or to anyone else. It doesn't make any difference. So the hell with it! I'll do whatever I want, whenever I want!" This fear of rejection will block an area of your emotional development, namely, the natural stage of maturation at the age of three. Three is the age when a child should naturally acquire the feeling of **responsibility**. If you bypassed this stage, you will act without consideration for anyone else and even for your own future. Instant gratification becomes your only way of life. This is the sine qua non of criminal behavior.

Infants have no patience, no compassion, no pity, no consideration—their only motivation is the immediate gratification of their needs regardless of the consequences to Mother or to any other person. If a newborn's mother dies, at that instant, it is of no importance to the infant as long as his or her needs are satisfied by a substitute parent. Newborns learn that if they cry loud and long enough, if they create enough commotion, somebody will feed them and satisfy their physical needs, they will survive. This is also true of the typical behavior of criminals, with the addition that criminals consider their **wants** to be the same as their **needs**.

Teenagers with this personality arrest of *early infancy*, characterized by feelings of **worthlessness**, consistently exhibit total disregard of their families' welfare and well-being. When they are in crisis or under pressure, the most you can expect from them is infantile behavior. They are indeed potential criminals; totally lacking a sense of responsibility, they will rationalize their actions, attitudes, and behavior without the slightest feeling of remorse or twinge of conscience; as they grow older, they may move from juvenile delinquency to full-fledged criminal behavior—theft, assault, and even murder.

Wife beating—an all-too-frequent expression of infantile uncontrolled anger—has occurred in America for over three hundred years, but only in very recent times has it been brought to widespread attention and disapproval. The courts are now willing to recognize that the wife beater has a fundamental emotional adjustment problem and often mandate that he receive professional help.

As an adult in the grip of the infantile personality arrest of worthlessness, you behave with *criminal disregard* for yourself and others. You don't care what happens to your spouse or children when you feel an urgent need to satisfy yourself. If you need a drink or gambling money, you will steal your spouse's money, or car, or whatever is available to do it. When you return home—often after driving drunk—and are no longer stressed, you may well say you are sorry and "won't do it again." Unless you allow yourself to mature emotionally, you will still be the same, no matter how well mannered or sophisticated you may act temporarily to carry out the con job on your family.

Infantile uncontrolled anger, ignited merely because you don't immediately "get your way," has no place in the family or in civilized society; without treatment, it can only grow worse until eventually, in a blind or drunken rage, someone gets killed.

## Child Beating

When you feel rejected, you respond with anger. If you felt rejected as an infant in your first year of life, you will develop one of the strongest kinds of emotional defense systems. Whenever you sense rejection—whether deliberate or unintentional—your response can be very violent, striking out at whomever or whatever is near. No matter what your size and age may be, you **behave as** an angry infant *in the first year of life*, striking out without regard for people and things around you. You can **act like** an adult as long as you don't feel rejected. But when you do feel rejected—whether this is true or not—you will respond with the violent defense you originally learned.

Take the case of a man successful and prominent in his job and the community. He is very aware of his economic success and feels himself socially respected. When the man relaxes over a couple of drinks at home at the end of the day, it becomes harder for him to maintain his adult pretenses. His infant son starts to cry, so the father orders him to shut up. The child becomes frightened and cries louder. The father feels that the child has no respect for him and is actually rejecting him.

The father reacts immediately to the perceived rejection with the defense he learned as a young infant. His anger is so overpowering and his reaction so quick that he starts shaking his son with no conscious thought or concern for the consequences. The son goes into a howling panic, which the father perceives as an even greater rejection than before; he reacts with increased violence by hitting the child. Both father and son are behaving at the infantile level, but the father is strong and coordinated, while his son is weak and helpless. If the child survives the father's assaults, years later he in turn will likely become a child beater himself.

The infant son cried out of need for attention, but received a violent rejection. His unsatisfied need for nurturing will remain throughout his life. His fear of rejection will be such that he will be unable to give or to receive acceptance and to form true, intimate human relationships.

## IRRITABILITY

As a newborn infant, long before you learn to speak, your ability to communicate *non*verbally is at an all-time high. You express your pleasure, curiosity, satisfaction, or delight—and your discomfort, hunger, dissatisfaction, anger, or alarm—through a full range of sounds and body signals. You babble, giggle, or gurgle and smile or grin; you cry or scream and frown, scowl, or purse your lips; you stare wide-eyed and grab, poke, or slap; you cringe or squirm and push away; you stretch and wiggle your fingers and toes; you wriggle and thrash or flail.

Your parents, however, may be so concerned about doing everything the "right way" and "on schedule" that they have neither the inclination nor the emotional energy to tune in to what you are telling them—to understand how you feel, what you want, and what you don't want. They ignore or disregard your sounds and signals. They don't feed you or hold you when you cry out to be fed or held—and they feed or hold you when you squirm and push away to be left alone.

Although these slights make you angry, you fear you will be rejected or abandoned if you express your anger openly and fully. You feel it is safer instead to get your needs satisfied by being fussy or cranky. Used repeatedly, successfully, and over prolonged periods of time, your low-grade anger becomes the *newborn* emotional defense of irritability.

## CRAVING FOR PHYSICAL CONTACT: SMOKING, COMPULSIVE SEX

When you are first born, you have an intense need to be touched and held. In the womb you were warm and protected and your skin was in extensive, intimate contact with your mother. Now you are out in the cold. At birth you need to be held immediately. If, as a newborn, you aren't touched and made to feel warm, you may have an insatiable, lifelong craving for close physical contact.

When smoking becomes a compulsive habit, it is likely to be a replay of your desire to be touched or stroked as an infant. You **behave as** a *newborn before the age of one* when you are smoking. You have an immense need for immediate gratification, without which you feel you could die—puffing on your cigarette is the most important thing you can do at that minute, and you simply aren't concerned about the future consequences. The warm smoke is mildly irritating and stimulating to one of the most sensitive parts of your body: the mucous membrane of your lips, mouth, and throat. Cigarettes are there when you reach out for them; they won't put you down or reject you.

As adults, we know how compelling the need for human contact can be, and how hard it is to satisfy. As infants before the age of one, most of us weren't held, touched, or stroked as much as we needed to be. This goes a long way toward explaining the large number of professional touchers, such as massagers, chiropractors, hairdressers, and the like. And it also explains why many men and women engage in compulsive sex—more out of an infantile craving for physical contact than in search of orgasmic response.

## SHUT-OFF FEELINGS: EMOTIONAL COLDNESS

You are born needing and expecting to be accepted as you are. After experiencing a series of rejections, deliberate or unintentional, you begin to drop some of the conscious aspects of this essential human expectation, but your basic need for acceptance will be with you all your life.

As a small baby, you need nourishment and physical protection—at least enough to allow you to live and become an adult. But for complete emotional development, your need for acceptance is just as urgent. During the *first twelve months* of life you need at least one person to give you love and care. You also need to feel that at least someone is tuned into your needs and longings. If you don't receive that intimacy—or receive too little—you in all likelihood will shut down part or almost all of your openness to love.

When, as an infant, you desperately wanted and needed the experience of shared intimacy and it wasn't provided you, you felt so hurt that you adopted your own posthypnotic suggestion—"Who needs it anyway?"—which still operates in you as an adult. With this defense, emotional openness and the willingness to share intimacy are likely to remain shut down until the arrest is recognized, acknowledged as necessary in the past, and released.

Emotional withdrawal is a very common problem found in all degrees of severity. Because of the deep-seated fear behind such withdrawal, it is one of the hardest problems to deal with therapeutically. Emotionally withdrawn persons, often simply considered "emotionally cold," may adequately and successfully take their places in society, but they will suppress any open expression of love and will be fearful of receiving love and making commitments.

## AGE ONE

At age one you are getting up and about. You can roll over, sit up, stand, and walk on your own. Fascinated by your surroundings, you reach out and move toward the world around you, touching, exploring, playing with what you find —and claiming it as yours. You learn to use your voice to get attention and to say your first words. You want to be noticed, talked to, and held—but only when *you* want to. By one and a half you become more demanding—wanting what you want *now*.

## THE SPOILED CHILD

If, as a *one-year-old* infant, you got almost anything you wanted, you became a spoiled child, demanding that others cater to your whims. If, as an adult, you still demand that others respond to you the way your parents did, you have an infantile (one-year-old) personality arrest. Somewhere you learned that, by demanding, you could get others to do everything for you—while giving nothing in return. Your doting parents hoped or believed you would accept and love them for giving into all of your wants. The real motivation for their behavior was their fear of rejection; they tried to buy your love and approval through constant appeasement.

With this excess attention from your parents comes an unwanted burden. As you grow older, you learn that your parents depend on you far too much for their emotional well-being. Even as an adult, you don't want to be responsible for anyone else's emotional well-being. How much more of a burden was it when you were eighteen months old and just beginning to learn to care for yourself as an individual? This impossible responsibility will cause you to resent and eventually to reject your parents—and anyone who emotionally resembles them.

There is almost a set formula for your development as a spoiled child. Your father or mother (or both parents) first earned their place and identity by being the good little boy or the good little girl, by doing everything right to gain *their* parents' approval. When they married, they then earned their identity by being the dutiful husband or wife, by doing everything to gain—and nothing to jeopardize—their spouse's approval. When you were born, they again shifted their need for approval, from spouse to baby, doing everything possible for you in the hope that you would love them. They didn't dare say no to any of your infantile demands for fear you might disapprove of them. You were taught, since infancy, that you deserved everything with no attached responsibility (as all infants do), and therefore, as an adult, you live with that handicap. You have harbored a deep resentment toward your father or mother (or both parents), because unconsciously they required you—from infancy—to be responsible for their happiness. Later in life, your parents wonder why you don't come to visit them.

## OVEREATING: OBESITY

Obesity is a complex syndrome because of the vast array of contributing factors. Many components of this syndrome are found in the defenses and conditioning of *one-year-old* infants. Of all the things you can do as an infant, what is guaranteed to get approval of your parents? Smiling is one, but the all-time winner is eating all the food provided for you.

If you were an unwanted child, your crying, wet diapers, and perhaps your very presence were a burden to your parents. But almost certainly you got approval for eating all your food. Maybe all you wanted was three ounces of milk, but the bottle held five ounces, so you got approval only when you finished all there was.

Eating is commonly equated with health: "Eat this, it will make you strong" or "Clean your plate, you need this to grow." However well-intentioned, these commands turn out to be devastating.

Studies show that the 2 billion fat cells we are born with normally increase to 20 to 30 billion by the age of twenty. But if we are force-fed as infants, our fat cells can be induced to multiply up to *100* billion. Children with this elevated number of fat cells are handicapped for life—they will always have great difficulty managing their weight and figure.

Common birth weight is seven to eight pounds, which triples in the first year, to about twenty-two pounds. From age one to two, however, the natural rate of weight gained slows markedly: if allowed to eat only when hungry, an infant gains no more than eight pounds, as a result of a lessened need for food and therefore lessened appetite. Parents, mostly for their own peace of mind, often think their infants should be eating a steadily increasing amount of food. They require their babies to eat even though they are full and fat, and the babies feel they must go along to gain their parents' approval.

As an adult, the more insecure you are, the more you need approval from others. To win this approval, you may well return to the survival technique that saved you as an infant—overeating. Your need to eat is most compelling when you feel rejected or unloved.

Other eating problems can be traced to early survival techniques such as "Eat to live" or "Eat to be big" (a small child doesn't distinguish fat from tall—both are "big"). The lack of proper nutrition, irregular feeding, the fear of starving, and the need to have something satisfying in the mouth (to nurse at Mother's breast) all relate to the need for affection. Take "nervous eating" for example. The nervousness can be traced to the agitation and insecurity of a fearful infant, usually between the ages of one and two, and the hang-up itself to the infant's survival techniques.

Hunger for food (appetite) is a basic biological drive. Eating is naturally limited by the satiety reflex: the *end* of hunger (**satiety**) is your body's signal you have eaten enough. When you eat *beyond* the point you no longer feel hungry, you are *over*eating. And when you eat until you feel *full*, you are *grossly* overeating. The feeling of fullness is your body's signal not only that you have eaten *more* than enough but that you are now storing food in your fat reserve. If hunger and satiety were allowed to function as natural processes, there would be little or no obesity. You can gain excessive weight only by eating when you *aren't* truly hungry. Sweetening baby food only induces babies to overeat, that is, to eat when they aren't really (physiologically) hungry.

As parents, we can quite easily gauge when our infant children are hungry and when they have eaten as much as they possibly can—that is, when they have clearly overeaten. Most of us, however, find it very hard to gauge when our children have eaten *enough*. Responding to the satiety reflex, infants simply *stop* eating when they are no longer hungry—their body's natural signal they have eaten enough. But as anxious, concerned, or insistent parents, we tend to ignore or disregard this response. Instead, we press our children to eat what *we* or the experts we rely on (including *our* parents) determine is enough for them. We urge them to override their basic feeling—until they become so full they resist any further efforts on our part to make them eat still more. Our children rightly resent this intrusion and interpret it as disapproval or rejection.

One of the most common associations that parents establish with their baby is the firm connection between sweets and acceptance. When you are an infant and your parents want you to like or accept them, they will often give you something sweet like candy, cookies, or ice cream. Later, the association is reinforced by your grandparents, uncles, or aunts, who also offer you something sweet like candy when they want you to like them. This is a ploy, unfortunately all too successful, that child molesters use to lure their young victims. Indeed, so strong does the association between sweets and acceptance become that, as a grown-up, one of the first things you may think of giving someone you want to like or accept you is candy.

It has been estimated that one out of every four American adults is "dangerously overweight." This widespread obesity can be traced to the suppression or emotional conversion of the automatic drive and reflex of hunger and satiety in the first three years—and unusually in the second year (*age one*)—of life. By earnestly and consistently overfeeding their babies, by teaching them to *consciously override* satiety—the end of hunger that is the natural signal to stop eating—parents are creating in their children the lifelong compulsion to overeat. Babies are also taught to include other needs into hunger, with the result that most of us confuse hunger for food with hunger for other needs. As with other personality arrests, the earlier you learn to override satiety and to confuse physical with emotional hunger, the stronger the personality arrest becomes, and the harder it is to release.

I believe that in almost all cases people become obese by eating when they aren't truly hungry. Every time you eat beyond satiety—when you are no longer hungry—you have overeaten. There are very few cases where obesity is actually due to an abnormal metabolic condition.

To overcome your tendency to overeat, you need to tune into your body and sort out your real need for nourishment from your emotional needs. The first step is to eat very slowly so that you become aware of your body's *natural* signals before you override them. Chew thoroughly and take at least twenty minutes to eat each meal. Next, you need to identify feelings *other* than hunger that have been stressful but that you have satisfied with the pleasurable experience of eating.

Overeating is rooted deeply in your subconscious mind and self-image. Any attempt to diet without addressing the underlying causes for overeating is only an attempt by your conscious mind to impose new controls on your subconscious mind—and therefore almost certain to fail. In a contest between your conscious and your subconscious mind you can expect your subconscious, with its drive to ensure your survival, to be the winner. For a diet to succeed, you need first to change your *feelings*—your *subconscious* mind—about food and eating.

Should you choose to reestablish these basic signals in your life—hunger (for food) as your signal to eat and satiety (end of hunger) as your signal to stop eating—you may at first experience feelings of panic. As an infant in need of acceptance, you learned how to dull satiety and to distort overeating into a self-rewarding and comforting activity. Through **directed age reenactment**, you can trace the emotional defense back to its origin (the initial sensitizing event) and uncover the circumstances that first led you to consciously override satiety and overeat. Working with an understanding friend, a counselor, or a support group will help you cope with your feelings of panic as you move through the six necessary steps to release your defenses about eating:

1. *Recognize that you have an eating problem.* Realize that will power alone (your conscious mind) cannot overcome it. Your tendency to overeat—to become fat or overweight—is a lifelong condition. What you do about it depends entirely on changing the way you *feel* about yourself (your unconscious mind).

2. *Reenact the time as an infant you first learned this emotional defense.* With the help of a therapist trained in directed age reenactment, return to the age you first felt you absolutely had to eat all you were given to be accepted, even though you weren't hungry. Reenact the first time you knew that if you didn't eat it all, you would be rejected or abandoned and you would die. Reexperience all the feelings you felt then.

3. *Acknowledge that your emotional defense was necessary at that time.* Recognize that, as an infant in need of acceptance, you had no other choice but to overeat.

4. *See the wounded infant within you.* Project yourself outside your body and look back at the wounded infant inside you trying to get acceptance by overeating. As this infant, you are "good" because you eat all your food, even when you aren't hungry, even when you are completely full. As this infant, you have learned to accept food in place of the love you need. Let your adult self understand, comfort, and reassure your infant self.
5. *Realize that, as an adult on your own, you no longer need your defense.* Acknowledge that you are safe and fine without it. You no longer have to eat when you aren't hungry to be accepted or loved. You are free to let go of your infant self's fear.
6. *Seek support from others in overcoming your problem.* Find a safe place with a good friend, counselor, or support group, where you will be understood rather than judged or excused, as you learn to accept your feelings and to put them in perspective.

## SEXUAL INHIBITIONS, MODESTY, POOR BODY IMAGE

Many people have deep sexual inhibitions, which they have attempted to deal with but failed. Some of these inhibitions come from the experiences and lessons learned as *one-year-old* infants, when they were forced to try to control some of their bodily functions before they were physically ready to.

Over the first six years of life, you learn to coordinate and refine your body's motions. This is a natural growth process and, because the nervous system is not fully developed at birth, cannot be accelerated, except to a minor degree. Many nerves, especially those controlling the entire genital-urinary-rectal area, have not yet grown their myelin sheath, which serves to insulate them, much as plastic coating insulates electrical wires. Because of this, your perception of sensations in areas served by these nerves, and your motor control of muscles governed by them, are generally unrefined, and will remain so until you reach the age of one and a half or two.

As a one-year-old infant, you could move your arms and shoulders, but you could not coordinate the fine movements of your hands. You had only the slightest control of your legs and feet and virtually no control over your processes of elimination.

When your mother or father demanded that you hold your urine or "go potty" on command, you tried your best to accommodate them. When you were less than one and a half, the best you could do was a regional "let go" and a regional "hold back."

If your mother's or father's demand, however expressed by word, deed, or gesture, was one of extreme urgency, you perceived that meeting their demand was vital to your survival. An angry parent four to five times bigger than you can be very threatening, but the feeling of rejection is much more damaging.

As a one-year-old, you could have been in a real bind when your angry or impatient parent sat you on a potty to urinate. If you sensed your parent's tension, you may have found it impossible to relax and therefore to urinate. Fifteen minutes later, when you went back to playing and relaxed—so did your urinary sphincter. Your mother or father may well have scolded you for being such a willful child. This lesson, if often repeated, will remain in your subconscious mind for a lifetime.

You shaped up by arresting your normal development of discriminating, finely tuned genital-urinary-rectal reflexes and responses. You did this by suppressing them *all at once*—by imposing regional control. Now, as an adult, you can't let go completely to a full orgasmic response because of the fear you subconsciously associate with letting go of urinary or rectal reflexes in the same region.

If in addition, when Father or Mother diapered you, they repeatedly showed any degree of revulsion or displeasure, this was transmitted to you, making you feel ashamed of that region of your body or of your entire body and leading to feelings of excessive modesty and physical or sexual inadequacy in later life. Their attitude subconsciously became part of your belief system, and you are likely to pass this same message to your own children and grandchildren.

We come into this world accepting all parts of our bodies without prejudice or repulsion. But the attitude our parents have about our physical characteristics can alter, limit, or reverse that acceptance. If your parents regard a part of your body as shameful or inadequate, you will react by adopting the same attitude and feelings. If, on the other hand, your parents exaggerate their praise of one part of your body to compensate for their disapproval of another, you will sense their disapproval beneath the exaggerated praise—and again you will adopt it as your own, feeling excessively modest or embarrassed about your body or appearance into your adult years.

What children need from their parents is acceptance of their bodies, their minds, and all of themselves, just for being —not as collections of great, good, not-so-good, and bad parts. If as a teenager or adult you are overly concerned with your physical appearance, even when everyone else thinks you look fine, then you need to uncover the fear that was implanted in you as an infant, typically *around the age of one*, when you were made to believe there was something wrong with you physically.

## STEALING

Stealing can be traced back to the age when it is perfectly normal for children to take things that don't belong to them. As soon as they can walk—when they are *about one year old*—toddlers "steal" all day long, that is, they pick up whatever fascinates them. Such behavior is understandable in infants less than one and a half years old, but if it continues *beyond* infancy, there is a problem.

When older children or adults steal, they are **behaving as** one-year-old infants for whom the only important thing is to satisfy their immediate wants, with total disregard for the owners. Their rationalizations are totally immaterial. If you, in turn, justify their theft in any way, you become part of the problem.

### CODEPENDENCY

Most often spouses of alcoholics have an emotional hang-up comparable to the alcoholics themselves, deeply rooted in a subconscious feeling of helplessness. They **act like** they deserve the repeated embarrassment, humiliation, and even beatings they receive from their alcoholic mates. They **behave as** *one-year-old* infants who still feel they need the support of their parents to survive, no matter what—that it is better to be abused than abandoned. This infantile need causes them to come back to the (parent) spouse again and again in spite of the abuse. As emotional one-year-olds, the only thing they truly understand is that they have a tested, successful survival technique—a defense that they have used many times in the past and that has allowed them to reach their current age. Before they can upgrade their self-image of helplessness and renounce their masochistic behavior, they need to find a safe place, such as an Alanon support group or a women's shelter for battered and abused women and children, where they can allow themselves to let down their defenses and begin the process of healing.

## AGE TWO TO TWO AND A HALF

During your first two years, you have very little influence or direction over your life. Your parents sit you up, lay you down, poke food in your mouth, and remove your soiled diapers. By the time you reach the age of two, however, you have learned to walk and run and to say no.

The phrase "terrible twos" is often used to describe a child's first concerted efforts to establish his or her separate identity. If you are thwarted in your attempt to be an individual—separate from your parents—you will remain a perennial two-year-old.

At two, you likely ran from place to place, touching and exploring everything. This is the age when your inborn curiosity and enthusiasm can be dampened, suppressed temporarily, or severely impaired. If yours was a highly structured home and your actions created too much disruption and distraction, your parents and older siblings may have reacted defensively by putting you down, thereby preventing you from exploring, touching, and acting out. The only defense available to you was to suppress your individuality and exploratory drive until you could feel safe enough to express them. Because your drive to establish your separate identity is basic and can only be delayed in its expression, your persistent efforts to subdue it may well have resulted in an explosion of rebellious activity in your early teenage years. The more repression you felt when you were two, the more your need for self-expression, for doing it "your own way" throughout your life.

If, as an adult, you insist on doing things entirely your own way without the benefit of advice or the experience of others, you are **behaving as** an infant *between two and two and a half* fighting for your separate identity but never feeling you have achieved it. By doing things "your own way" without help, you are trying to prove to yourself—without ever believing it—that you are an individual separate from everyone else, competent on your own. If you don't feel that you gained your individuality at the age of two, you will try to do so for the rest of your life.

The world is full of two-year-olds, which is not all bad. They can bring new approaches to old problems and often help to develop new tools and improved techniques.

I identify myself as a two-year-old, for when I was two, my older siblings were always telling me "how things should be done." I was rarely allowed to figure things out for myself.

Later, I found the way my peers were managing tasks—solely as they were taught—far too constrictive. Writing this book is an example of doing things "my own way." As a dyslexic, I knew from the beginning how much added effort it would take to write down my thoughts, page by page, chapter by chapter.

Research has determined that, because of slower transit time through the electrical connections in their brains, dyslexics take longer to recognize numbers and letters. This confirms what I experienced from the time I first started to read. Years later, when I would go shopping with my wife, she could preview everything on the whole aisle while I was still scanning the first shelf. This also explains the difficulty I had when using a stethoscope in medical school. No matter how hard I tried, I couldn't distinguish the precise timing of a heart murmur, which needs to be detected in the one to three milliseconds before the normal (lub-dub) sound of the heartbeat. Dyslexics are like the singing-impaired, who may love to sing, but because of the wiring in their brains, the usual feedback circuitry doesn't signal them soon enough when they are off pitch. Although dyslexia is a real handicap, I believe it has its compensations—mainly, it lets me make associations that nondyslexic persons can't make between highly diverse subjects.

## DEFIANCE

Although it serves as a primary life-saving force when you are born, and may later be useful in certain limited contexts, anger—whether expressed directly in response to genuine threats or defensively in response to imagined ones—is almost always detrimental to social interactions. How much anger you feel, and how easily it can be provoked, depends on how well you learned to use anger to satisfy your needs and wants in infancy and childhood.

When your parents or older siblings urge or order you, as an infant *between two and two and a half*, to do something your intuition tells you not to, you automatically say no. If they persist and repeatedly press you to do things you feel compromise your integrity, and if that makes you angry enough to defy their authority, you protect yourself by forming the infantile emotional defense of defiance.

## SELFISHNESS

As an infant (before the age of two and a half), your concern for others is limited to what they can do for you. You are in no position to do anything for them. Indeed, intent on surviving and establishing your own identity, you care little about your effect on others. Selfish behavior is rooted in this infantile reaction to life. As an infant *between two and two and a half*, you have no concept of the future, therefore you aren't willing to delay satisfaction of your wants for a future gain. Your whole existence is the here and now—what you want, you must have right now. How many times have you seen this impatient, self-centered, infantile behavior in an adult?

If you are selfish as an adult, it is because during the first two and a half years of life you were many times put in a position where you felt abandoned and feared for your life. As a two-year-old, your perception was that you saved yourself each time by grabbing on to anything or anybody. As a selfish adult, you continue to **behave as** a fearful two-year-old who must demand attention or take things in order to survive. When formed earlier, at *age one or before*, this infantile personality arrest is evident in the intense, often criminal selfishness characteristic of most of the prison population.

## EVASIVENESS: RUNNING AWAY

The emotional defense of evasiveness may be manifested at any stage in life, but it belongs to the utterly frustrated infant *between two and two and a half*.

At two, you no longer have the infantile instinct of blindly striking out or hitting back, and yet you haven't fully developed your reasoning or vocal skills to protest effectively. You do have feet under you and have learned to run; consequently, in frustration, you may rush off blindly in any direction, not knowing where you are going. As a two-year-old, you aren't concerned about consequences. You just want to get away. As a teenager, you may have been frustrated enough to become a runaway.

You often see this evasive behavior in teenagers and in parents, who, because of their frustration and inability to communicate, run away from each other—literally or in effect. Your boss or your spouse may "run away" without even leaving the room by becoming evasive, by repeatedly ignoring complaints or by changing the subject whenever issues that make them uncomfortable are raised. Make no excuse, they are all **behaving as** frustrated infants *between two and two and a half.*

## PROFANITY

Spoken in anger, profanity can be a normal behavior for an infant between two and two and half who has already learned by example from his or her parents how to express anger by swearing. When adults use profanity, however, most often they are **behaving as** angry, frustrated infants *between two and two and a half* unable to express their frustration in any other way.

On my first day of internship in a New England hospital, I was making my rounds of the pediatric ward. There in a crib stood a second-generation, two-year-old Italian boy, shaking the crib bars and cursing at me in Italian. He was uncomfortable, angry, and frustrated and had no other way to express his plight.

Now when I hear angry profanity, I again hear and see that two-year-old infant.

## FRIGIDITY

Suppose you are a little girl between two and two and a half years old and you feel warm, open, and loving. What you want most is to be touched, held, and loved. Being warm and loving will be an essential part of your sexuality in later life. Suppose also that your father and mother are busy when you approach them and they tell you, "Don't bother me now." You feel you are being pushed away. If this happens not just once, but again and again, you protect yourself from this rejection by not allowing yourself to be emotionally open and receptive. Formed *between two and two and a half* and reinforced over time, the emotional defense of frigidity, which typically manifests itself as cold hands, cold feet, dry lips, and muscular tightness in the body, can impair or completely block your ability to either receive or express love and affection.

When you become sexually active, your fear of intimacy will make it difficult for you to reach full, mature sexual expression. You may use an unpleasant or distasteful sexual encounter to justify your lack of sexuality. It is highly likely, however, that the encounter subconsciously reminded you of your traumatic rejection as a two-year-old. Until you overcome that two-year-old's fear of closeness, you won't be able to feel comfortable enough to become physically and emotionally intimate with another.

Often while conducting an age reenactment with a female patient, I notice the patient's hands become suddenly cold and sweaty. When I call her attention to this reaction, she is often able to reconstruct—reenact—the scene of her childhood, about the age of two, where she is seeking closeness with her parents but is being pushed away. She can now feel and describe her mother's or father's attitude—and her own reaction. The defense she learned then to protect herself so that she would never again be placed in that vulnerable spot—unless recognized, acknowledged as necessary *then*, and released—can last for the rest of her life.

## ALCOHOLISM AND OTHER SELF-DESTRUCTIVE BEHAVIOR

When I ask my alcoholic patients to assign themselves what they feel is their proper place in a row of all the people they know, with the most worthy at one end and the least worthy at the other, they invariably place themselves at the least worthy end of the row.

If you believe you are "unworthy," if this becomes your self-image, then you feel you deserve nothing good and are compelled to behave accordingly. When you are small, and your parents, on whom you are dependent for your very existence, let you feel by word, deed, or attitude that you are unworthy, you believe them, and you predicate your life on assuming the role they have cast for you.

This role requires you as a child, usually about the age of two, to keep a low profile or suffer harsh punishment. Throughout the first six years of your life, by such repeated reprimands as "Shame on you!" or "Don't you care about anyone but yourself?" or "Won't you ever learn?" you become afraid of any accomplishments or actions that might cause your parents or older siblings to feel threatened. When you display more mature behavior than your parents, they indeed feel threatened and hostile toward you, for their own behavior is more childish. As a two-year-old infant, you acutely feel their hostility. Needing to believe they are superior to you, your parents or older siblings may call you foul names, ridicule you, and repeatedly berate you for not doing anything "the way you are supposed to"—the way *they* do. You, in turn, accept and assume the role of unworthy infant from that time forward—and probably for the rest of your life. Your ingrained feeling is that they (your parents, older siblings) won't allow you (the infant) to live feeling any other way about yourself.

When, as an infant *between two and two and a half*, you are made to feel unworthy, you have a strong tendency to avoid any possibility of long-term achievement. You do everything you can to get yourself out of any favorable position (reverting to that low profile). Being the most you can be will threaten those around you and bring certain punishment or rejection. Even as a two-year-old, you compete for attention or love with the older people in your life—and thereby threaten them. Because you depend on them for everything, displeasing them could mean total rejection of you.

Later, as an older child, on occasions when you adopt the role of parent for your younger siblings, you then feel threatened by them (just as your parents or older siblings did by you), particularly if the younger children surpass you in emotional maturity and sometimes in physical size and capability.

As you grow older, you may well **behave as** "the brat" when people are being good to you. You turn around and kick them in the shins to retain the identity you learned as a younger child and to return to the safety of your status quo. Your self-image is based on the premise that you are unworthy, therefore when anyone shows you kindness or what you take for special consideration, it frightens you. Not knowing how to deal with this unfamiliar situation, you revert back to what you did to save your life as a very small child—you play the unworthy infant.

You can identify the alcoholic in a group of first graders because his or her feeling of **unworthiness**, rooted between the ages of two and two and a half, expresses itself so strongly. And later, when children start to drink, you can identify self-destructive or alcoholic drinking almost immediately. Junior high school students who repeatedly say, "I'm going to go out and get drunk," have a drinking problem. When they drink, not two beers, but two six-packs, enough to become socially obnoxious, they are exhibiting self-destructive or alcoholic behavior. Formed earlier, *before the age of one*, this infantile personality arrest is apparent in adults who feel not just unworthy but actually *worthless*—in alcoholics who show *criminal* disregard for others or themselves. Like those who are addicted to hard or mind-altering drugs, alcoholics who repeatedly drive while drunk, who physically and emotionally abuse others when drunk yet drink anyway, and who continue to drink despite clear signs they are destroying their health are almost certain to have learned this more deeply rooted defense of **worthlessness** before they reached the age of one. Believe what you see, make no excuses for anyone.

Just because you feel unworthy doesn't automatically make you an alcoholic. You may find other ways to behave self-destructively—by gambling, driving recklessly, or simply by starting good relationships or promising careers and then subconsciously sabotaging them; in other words, by destroying what you profess you most earnestly desire. Like the alcoholic, you **behave as** an "unworthy" infant *between two and two and a half.*

## SUMMARY

As an infant, and even in your mother's womb, you react to repeated threats by forming potentially lifelong **emotional defenses—personality arrests**. These range from mild hang-ups to full-blown psychosis, depending on the severity and frequency of the threats and your age at the time you formed your defenses against them. Thus, **claustrophobia** and **schizophrenia** arise from defenses formed before birth; craving for physical contact, violent temper, irritability, and shut-off emotions—birth to age one; spoiled behavior, overeating, sexual inhibitions, stealing, and codependency—age one to two; and defiance, selfishness, evasiveness, habitual profanity, frigidity, and alcoholism—age two to two and a half.

The three chief factors in releasing your personality arrests—or preventing them in your children—are **awareness**, **learning**, and **knowledge**. Awareness begins only when you stop explaining or justifying your behavior—and the behavior of your children—and see it exactly as it *is*. To change the behavior of your children, you need to change your own behavior, and therefore also your *feelings* about yourself—your **self-image**.

First, identify the behavior you wish to change and, referring to the Smith Index (pages 24–25), age-date it. Next, find a safe place with an understanding friend, counselor, or support group where you can discuss your observations and share your feelings about this behavior (emotional defense). Then, with the help of a therapist trained in **directed age reenactment**, *reexperience* the circumstances that first led you to form your defense (the **initial sensitizing event**). Finally, bring all you have experienced and learned since you were an infant or child (your learning)—and all you intuitively *know* to be true (your knowledge)—to bear on that event and your feelings about it. Do this again and again, until you release your **fear** or **anger** and the defense you formed as a result.

To rear your children free from the fears and anger that give rise to personality arrests, you need to begin while they are still in their **infancy** (birth to age two and a half), before they take on the challenges of **childhood** (ages two and a half to six). You need to understand the dynamics of emotional development and to be in tune with your children's feelings. Above all, you need to be not only aware of your fears, anger, and personality arrests but in tune with your *own* feelings.

# 4

# CHILDHOOD

## Two and a Half to Six Years of Age

### AGE TWO AND A HALF TO THREE

When you are born, you are the center of your universe. You consider no one but yourself, your survival—your pleasure or your displeasure. By the age of two and a half, you become aware of the people around you. With this awareness, you will later (between three a half and four and a half) develop a sense of responsibility towards others.

At two and a half, you still retain much of the sense of importance you had originally, but you begin to realize you must adjust to others in order to be part of the family, which in turn will continue to satisfy your needs. Your importance to others is not a given, but only what they *allow* it to be. If you don't feel threatened or rejected, you can make the adjustment smoothly; you can realize it is safe to relinquish your immediate demands and place trust in those around you.

On the other hand, your emotional growth can be arrested if your parents or older siblings take advantage of your two-and-a-half-year-old naïveté. They can invoke in you

—either indirectly through comparisons with other siblings or directly through criticism—a sense that you are the cause of the disharmony in the family. You may respond by becoming angry; to protect yourself, you become aggressive or passive aggressive. Or you may respond by absorbing the blame; to protect yourself, you become anxious, indecisive, or depressed—or you put on airs.

## AGGRESSIVENESS AND PASSIVE AGGRESSIVENESS

At two and a half, you are the embodiment of energy, initiative, and enthusiasm. If your parents repeatedly attempt to throttle your healthy self-assertion by manipulating or intimidating you—making you feel deficient and somehow the cause of the family's troubles—you may grow angry. If you are spunky enough, you may protect yourself from their encroachments by becoming aggressive, by encroaching on *other* people's rights and feelings—bending others to your will through manipulation and intimidation.

When you are an aggressive adult, you **behave as** an angry child *between two and a half and three* who hasn't developed the responsibility and respect for others characteristic of three-year-olds. You are like the aggressive salesman, who preys on your weaknesses and hang-ups to bully or pressure you into buying something you don't want, don't need, or can't even afford—as opposed to the *assertive* salesman, who actively listens, who perceives what you want and need, and who responds to and even anticipates your concerns.

If at two and a half you are angry but also afraid of being rejected or punished, you may learn to disguise your anger by becoming passive aggressive, pretending to comply with others' demands, while in fact doing nothing of the kind. If Mother tells you, "Brush your teeth," you may answer, "Okay, Mom," go into the bathroom, shut the door, run the water, play around, but never lift your toothbrush.

As a passive aggressive adult, you may, for example, go to your doctor's office with a severe case of strep throat. When the doctor tells you to be sure to take all the pills he has prescribed, you promise you will, then take only as many as you need to relieve your pain. Your throat heals in weeks instead of days; the rest of the pills end up on the top shelf of your medicine cabinet. You are **behaving as** a child *between two and a half and three*, angry at those making demands but afraid of being punished. You have learned instead to express your anger *in*directly, through the emotional defense of **passive aggressiveness**.

## ANXIETY, WORRY

Although it can be manifested at any age, anxiety—especially free-floating anxiety—is normally a *two-and-a-half-year-old* personality arrest. Anxiety is the readiness to act without direction, usually of short duration, accompanied by the fear that any move made will be the wrong one.

As a child between two and a half and three, you could sense when something was awry and life-threatening to your family. You weren't able to ask detailed questions, nor to understand their answers if you could, and no one was inclined to explain anything to you. Yet you were probably much more receptive to the feelings and emotions of those around you than they were. You didn't understand the cause of what was wrong, but you certainly felt the effect.

You wanted to run, but were too afraid to be separated from your parents and protectors. You felt trapped in a situation that you couldn't understand and that was out of your control, but that you had to endure. So you defended yourself the only way you knew how—you became anxious, you worried. Later in life, when a situation recalls that trapped feeling, you again experience unbridled fear, and you again **behave as** a helpless, anxious child *between two and a half and three*.

## INDECISIVENESS

Indecisiveness is a learned behavior that cannot be logically explained in terms of your current situation and that keeps you far below your full potential, whether financial or social. If you are indecisive, you act as though even a limited commitment will put you in a situation where you cannot escape. You **behave as** a fearful child *between two and a half and three* whose answers or decisions were unacceptable and whose self-image was devastated by parental condemnation and rejection.

Nobody wants to be indecisive, but it can become an emotionally necessary defense for a two-and-a-half-year-old. To be secure in your identity, to attain the maturity of a three-year-old, you need to feel that your ideas and decisions are considered and accepted or at least respected. Repeated rejection or ridicule of your decision-making efforts will result in a personality arrest at the age when decisions are made for you—two and a half to three. As an emotional two-and-a-half-year-old, you protect yourself from devastating condemnation and rejection the only way you know how, by refusing to make or hold to decisions—you become indecisive.

In our society, there are secure havens for the indecisive individual. You can join a group with a strong leader or hierarchy that has answers for every situation (like some fundamentalist sects or the military). Here you will be relieved of any responsibility; your leader, superior officer, or NCO, who functions in the same manner as Father did in your family, will make all necessary decisions for you and the other members of the group. Indeed, you may find yourself accepted *only if* you emotionally **behave as** a fearful two-and-a-half-year-old—by suppressing your natural curiosity and by accepting your (parent) leader's decisions without question.

## DEPRESSION

A feeling of emotional dejection deeper and more prolonged than warranted by any objective reason, depression is a *two-and-a-half-year-old* personality arrest. It comes and goes, lasting for quite a while or for a relatively short time. Depressed people are nearly always sad, gloomy, or listless; often their movements are slow, their concentration poor, and they have difficulty thinking or eating normally; their usual self-reliance is replaced by feelings of despair and uselessness. They **behave as** children *between two and a half and three*, blocked in their normal expression of exuberance and experimentation, who feel helpless and are afraid of doing or being anything—and who cannot explain why they feel the way they do about themselves.

If you are depressed, more than likely when you were two and a half to three, your family situation trapped you into a state of inactivity. At age two and a half, urgently needing your parents' acceptance but faced instead with their disapproval or rejection, you felt trapped, so you protected yourself the only way you knew how: you shut down your feelings, your expression, your activity—everything that might further displease your parents. In other words, you withdrew into depression. In your dreams, night after night, your subconscious will call forth images of the situation that first threatened you. Night after night, it will activate your defenses of emotional withdrawal, leaving you weary and emotionally flat each morning, and reinforcing your feelings of despair and uselessness.

## PRETENTIOUSNESS: PUTTING ON AIRS

As a child between two and a half and three, your identity was not yet fully established. If your parents or older siblings criticized you, put you down, or compared you unfavorably to other siblings, you may have developed feelings of inadequacy. To protect yourself against these feelings, you formed the emotional defense of pretentiousness—of putting on airs to show you were "better" (better looking, more grown-up, smarter, more serious) than they thought (or you felt) you were.

Teenagers and adults with this personality arrest of early childhood may use excessive makeup or display excessive concern about their appearance (hairstyle, jewelry, brand and style of clothes), often spending more than they can afford to look "better" than their peers, or affecting a style of speech that is more adult, more sophisticated, or more hip than they feel. But, in times of stress, they remain and **behave as** frightened children *between two and a half and three* who haven't yet reached the age of responsibility and who, no matter what they do, feel inadequate.

## AGE THREE

At three, you are clearly aware of who you are. Your feeling of self-importance is at an all-time high—the world is yours, you have control of it, and you want to be a part of everything around you. You tend to be rigid and ritualistic, at times bossy and demanding, determined to have your own way. Soon this will be tempered by a sense of responsibility, which you begin to develop between three and a half and four and a half. You are becoming aware that others have identities as well and that they are important to your survival. You take words very literally—they mean one thing and one thing only. You are beginning to think in logical ways, and your parents are beginning to listen to what you say.

### BLIND OBEDIENCE

At three, you begin to reason and analyze, to ask logical questions. If your parents reject you or put you down every time you attempt to use your inquiring mind, you defend yourself by accepting what they tell you as the absolute truth.

You become forever fearful of questioning or analyzing new ideas or beliefs.

People with the personality arrest of blind obedience **behave as** frightened *three-year-old* children blindly accepting whatever their parents or elders tell them as true. As adults, they think entirely in terms of the unshakable beliefs taught them by their leaders, whether political, social, or religious. You can't argue with people of this mind-set, for neither their belief system nor any particular belief within it is open to discussion.

The sect of charismatic religious leader Jim Jones in the 1970s is an extreme instance of blind obedience. Jones's followers gave up their jobs, their homes, and everything they owned in California to form a religious farming commune under his leadership in Guyana (formerly British Guiana), South America. All decisions and all control were vested in Jones. The commune appears to have been successful at first, and its blindly obedient members happy under this total "parental guidance." After a few years, however, because the individual decision-making drive can't be permanently suppressed, unrest began to grow. When it threatened Jones's leadership, rather than disband his group, he convinced (or coerced) nearly all of his eight hundred followers to join him in mass suicide.

## FAULT

To be at **fault**, you first have to assume that you have the power to make things right. As a three-year-old, you believe that *you can make the world right*. Remember some of your three-year-old sayings? "Walk on cracks, break you mother's back," "You squash bugs, you get rain." Superstition is a three-year-old's reaction and defense. The superstitious person **behaves as** a three-year-old child who believes everything he or she does affects the whole world, the sun, the moon and the course of history.

If, at three, you sense that something is wrong in your family, but your parents and older siblings won't say what, you become afraid you will be left out of your family altogether. So you defend yourself the only way you know how —you take on the "wrong"; in order to "make the world right" again, to be accepted back into your family, you become "at fault." As a *three-year-old*, when you feel you are at fault over a stressful situation that you did nothing to prevent or remedy (even though you weren't the cause), you assume a feeling of blame that can remain with you the rest of your life.

## GUILT

If as an adult you feel guilty, your family most likely turned your newly gained sense of responsibility against you by converting it to **guilt**. Your sense of guilt was created solely for the convenience of family manipulation. This guilt gave them a handle to readily control and dominate you, not just as a child, but throughout your life. If this personality arrest occurs when you are beginning to develop a sense of responsibility—*between three and a half and four and a half*— you may feel guilty all your life.

When others use the same guilt handle your family used to manipulate you, your self-image only gets lower and lower. Guilt demands punishment and this punishment or self-denial only further depreciates your sense of self-worth. Guilt is destructive because it keeps you in the past. To be truly safe, you must accept—approve of—yourself as you are. If you seek approval from others for what you are or do, you expose yourself to being manipulated and used. You are then willing to do or be whatever other people expect—without considering your own feelings, your own sense of worth. You are not safe in this world until you can choose to say no without feeling guilty.

Temporary guilt can serve a useful purpose by prodding you to recognize when you have acted in a manner *you* consider thoughtless, inconsiderate, or wrong—in time to do something about it. This damage control can help prevent a lifelong guilt complex. Otherwise, in its usual sense, guilt is completely negative; it is always for something in the past, and the past can never be changed (except to get a new understanding of the past). In place of guilt, you need to foster responsibility for the future. Responsibility is the opposite to guilt. A sense of responsibility comes naturally to a child between three and a half and four and a half years old. You need to restore this sense of responsibility for the future and make it applicable to your adult world.

## SHAME

Although related to guilt, **shame** can be more destructive. **Guilt** is a feeling originally induced by others to punish you for *doing* something they consider wrong (or for *not* doing something they consider right). In contrast, **shame**, while also induced by others, is designed to punish you for *being* someone others consider inferior (or for *not* being someone they consider superior). When this personality arrest occurs *around the age of three*, you may feel ashamed all your life.

When you do something quite natural for a child of three to three and a half, like running around naked, and your parents scold you severely, you defend yourself against rejection by blushing, falling silent, and feeling ashamed. If this happens repeatedly, you will carry this shame of your body into adulthood, making you always fearful of being naked in the presence of others, whether it be in a gym or an intimate situation.

Shame may also make you feel that you are carrying the burden of your family's secrets, that you have to bear the heavy load of your parents' or siblings' socially unacceptable traits (alcoholism, mental retardation, and the like). People attempt to cast shame on others they consider inferior purely to control and emotionally enslave them. There is no possible benefit for those who assume the shame.

## RIDDING YOURSELF OF FAULT, GUILT, AND SHAME

To grow to full emotional maturity, you need to completely rid yourself of fault, guilt, and shame. In their place, you need to encourage the growth of a healthy sense of responsibility. Fault, guilt, and shame are like parasites, which, if allowed to flourish, will sap your energy—or even cripple you emotionally.

You need to grant amnesty, first to yourself for having allowed these parasites to sap your vitality, and then to those who took advantage of you. Don't expect those who fostered fault, guilt, and shame in you to ever relax their attempts to dominate you. Expecting those who dominate you to change or set you free only proves that they still control you.

Any and all changes have to come from within you, for yourself alone. (If you are in a twelve-step program, you might ask your higher power to help you as you go about your healing.) Acknowledge that you were created as a being unique in your own right and that you belong here as much as every other being. There are no "right" or "wrong" people born into this world, we just are.

The cure for fault, guilt, and shame is the outright renunciation and rejection of the thought that you are responsible for the incapacities and deficiencies of others. To undo the damage: (1) *recognize* the defenses of fault, guilt, and shame in your patterns of behavior; (2) with the help of a therapist trained in directed age reenactment, *reexperience* the original incident—the sensitizing event—when you were first made to feel at fault, guilty, or ashamed; (3) *acknowledge* that such defenses were necessary and appropriate for that time—usually around the age of three—and place; (4) *imagine* your three-year-old self and, drawing on all you have learned since you were three, give this child self your adult knowledge and support—show your child there are *other* choices;

and (5) *help* your child self *release* the fears that have such a hold over you. Each time you call up this image of your three-year-old self, each time you help your child self, you reprogram your subconscious and upgrade your self-image. And each time, you let yourself mature emotionally toward healthy self-assertiveness.

## THE NICE PERSON

When you look at the nice baby, the nice toddler, the nice teenager, and the nice adult, what do they all have in common? They all conform to what is expected of them socially; they are all clean, quiet, or at least not disruptive, and exhibit only acceptable emotions at appropriate times. Usually we call people "nice" when they are well behaved and agreeable, but we can find nothing special or characteristic about them—they are "generic" people. If you are a "nice person," you get only the identity that other people give you, never your own unique identity.

If as an infant you felt rejected more often than not, by the age of three you had a low self-image. At three, when you still weren't accepted for who you were, you found that your family offered you great approval if you faithfully followed what they said and did everything the "right way"—your mother's or father's way—because to do or say anything your *own* way would cause your parents to disapprove.

As a three-year-old, the game of being "nice" saved your life many, many times. Consequently, you play the game the rest of your days. Furthermore, you want everyone around you to play it with you, not for their benefit, but for yours. As a "nice" adult, you are still **behaving as** the rejected *three-year-old* whose own ideas and feelings are unacceptable and whose only way to maintain parental approval is to act out the role they have ascribed to you.

## THE PERFECTIONIST

If you are a perfectionist, you will find that there is a great demand for your services in much of the business world, but little demand for them in a family whose members need close, personal, accepting relationships.

As an adult perfectionist, you are operating on a *three-year-old* emotional level. That was the time in your emotional development when you considered yourself the center of your world but were also aware that your surroundings had order and that you must conform to that order or be punished. You still **behave as** a fearful three-year-old who must have everything in its place and done properly or else be devastatingly rejected—and therefore die.

You feel yourself personally responsible for the actions of everyone around you. As a perfectionist, you are a guaranteed emotional loser. You can never get a project completed to your entire satisfaction. Even when you manage to spend the time necessary to do any job "correctly," you have to neglect other aspects of your life.

Your perfectionism imposes stringent restrictions on you and makes others uncomfortable to be around you. Inevitably, they sense your self-censure and interpret it as disapproval of them.

When you try to control those around you—to impose your perfectionist standards on them—their only defense is to move away from you whenever possible.

Two extreme forms of this *three-year-old* personality arrest are **kleptomania** and **anorexia nervosa**. Unlike one-year-olds' natural tendency to steal—to consider everything as belonging to them—which infants normally outgrow, kleptomaniacs' compulsive stealing is an emotional defense of rejected three-year-olds who see stealing as the only way they can be "right" for themselves. When kleptomaniacs steal again and again—most often not consciously aware they are stealing—they are **behaving as** rejected, frustrated *three-year-olds* desperately trying to establish their "rightness" for themselves by taking what belongs to others.

Likewise, anorexics' compulsive fasting is an emotional defense of rejected *three-year-olds* who see fasting as the only way to make themselves "right." Emotionally, anorexics (almost exclusively women) are nice little girls (or, rarely, boys) who lead carefully circumscribed lives and whose penmanship—carefully rounded, uniform letters with extenders only slightly above and below the mid-zone—reflects their constant striving for perfection and their need to control all risk in their lives. Through their compulsive fasting, anorexics try to make their overweight self-image conform to their slender, "perfect" ideal. No matter how thin they become, they always *feel* themselves to be fat. When they fast, they **behave as** anxious, fearful three-year-olds desperately trying to make themselves "right."

## THE CON ARTIST

If you are a con artist, as a *three-year-old* when you weren't accepted for what you were, you learned how to gain great approval from those about you. Much more aware of the feelings of others and possessing greater intuition than the average individual, you tune into your victim's feelings to serve your own ends. As a newborn infant with a beguiling smile and pleasing demeanor, you unconsciously ingratiated yourself with those around you. Now, after three years of experience, you consciously and deliberately smooth your path through life and refine your ways to "beat the system."

## FAIRNESS

You might not believe that attachment to the ideal of fairness is an emotional hang-up, but it is. Is it "fair" that you live in this country instead of a starving Third World nation? Is it "fair" to others that you are healthy and talented and they are not? How much of life do you really think is "fair"?

There is no fairness in nature, only natural order. Individual plants or animals are all required to adjust to the environment or perish. Nothing in human relationships is "fair" or equal, and it never will be.

Nevertheless, children invariably are taught that they must be "fair." This is pure fantasy. It is good to be caring, considerate, understanding, and responsible for your actions, but that is not fairness. Fairness, as well as truth, is a very individual and subjective concept. Although in everyday life students, workers, volunteers, and athletes who work face-to-face or in teams can display a good approximate sense of fairness, sharing responsibilities, rewards, and credit in an easy give-and-take, in general, people are likely to consider things to be "fair" only when they have a clear advantage over everyone else—or when the situation is the way they want it to be.

If as an adult, you persist in holding on to this mythical fairness, you are **behaving as** a frightened *three-year-old*, making yourself into a "victim" because you believe the whole world is against you. Consequently, you may withdraw into bitter isolation and be unable to use the many special advantages you possess. Or, on the other hand, you may react to this "unfair" world by becoming a social worker, a political or consumer activist, or by joining a cause that will encourage or support your fantasy of "fairness."

## JEALOUSY

When you are three years old, you want to be accepted as an equal member of the family. But, if the grown-ups around you constantly compare you to a brother or sister whom they find stronger, faster, brighter, handsomer, or prettier, you will accept this judgment, however much it makes you feel insecure and inadequate. When you are three and your sister is six, she is indeed taller, more dexterous, and more accomplished than you. You are painfully aware that this is so, that there is nothing you can do to be her equal. You defend yourself against being rejected and abandoned with the *three-year-old* personality arrest of jealousy—by feeling that you *cannot compete* successfully.

As a small child when you felt hurt by these comparisons, you might have run to your more sympathetic parent. If this parent soothed your hurt *without* accepting you as you were, this only served to reinforce your feelings of inadequacy—of jealousy—and you learned a protective behavior that can remain with you throughout your life.

A jealous adult is **behaving as** a hurt and insecure *three-year-old* child. Logic is no help here; you can only deal with him or her at that age level.

## SARCASM, BITTERNESS AND RESENTMENT

As adults, we use tone of voice and inflection to give our words different meanings from their usual senses. These variations are the basis for jokes as well as sarcasm. Humor and sarcasm have hurt or cruelty at their core; a twist or variation in the usual (literal) sense of words is designed to amuse and bring laughter. Children learn to apply the cruelty in humor by example. The one- or two-year-old acts without direction, but at three you begin to direct your attention and energies toward specific people.

As a three-year-old, you understand words very literally, just like your subconscious mind, which has only one meaning for each word. You seldom, if ever, understand jokes, laughing, or ridicule when the adults use you as the object of their laughter. You may invent games that cause you to laugh and giggle when your parents play with you, but when your mother or father laughs at you in ridicule, you can only withdraw in hurt. You defend yourself against that hurt with the *three-year-old* personality arrest of sarcasm. Later in life, you continue to use sarcasm and cutting remarks as an expression of your pent-up feelings of hurt and anger.

If as an infant you are cranky or fussy and if your parents put unrealistically high expectations on you, your low-grade anger may eventually become the personality arrest of bitterness and resentment. In later years, you continue to defend yourself by **behaving as** a bitter, resentful *three-year-old* whenever you feel put upon.

## AGE FOUR

At four, your personal identity is established and your critical judgment is up and running. You are ready to learn the working rules of your family or group, and you become fairly adept at whatever games they play. You mimic your older siblings, trying to do what they do. You are eager to help out within the limits of your attention span.

## LYING

When you first started to talk, between one and one and a half, you were allowed to babble on and blurt out whatever came spontaneously; as a small child, you were excessively truthful and said some shocking things or broadcast family secrets.

Now that you are four, you have to be careful to say the "correct thing," to tell your parents what they want to hear. As a frank and truthful child, you can cause your parents and older siblings embarrassment, which in turn may cause them to reject you. You discover that you need to become skillful at guessing what the grown-ups in your life expect to hear, rather than the truth as you know it. You are required to tell so many lies that lying becomes your way of life. Each time you lie, your confidence in your own intuition, and therefore also your **self-esteem**, is diminished.

Probably one of the most damaging questions your parents can ask you is *why*? *Why* is a legitimate question in philosophy or engineering or to find out what makes your bank statement out of balance, but it has no place in understanding human emotions or defenses.

"Why did you take that cookie?" is a fine question if Mother or Father is prepared to accept an honest answer—obviously, you took the cookie because you felt like it. "Why didn't you wash your hands?"—because you didn't feel like it. But these answers, however honest, aren't likely to be accepted by either of your parents.

The effect of their asking you *why* is to put you on the defensive. If every time you tell the truth, your parents get upset and scold you, you quickly learn to make something up. The *only* purpose of asking children *why* is to *teach them to lie*.

In our culture, children are raised to tell lies in all kinds of situations. There are expected, "correct" answers in the playground, at Grandma's, or when guests come to visit. As a four-year-old, you aren't allowed to say what you intuitively know to be true. You must tell others what they *expect* to hear, however untrue. Later, as an adult, you will reward, with your vote or your purchase, people whose job it is to tell you what *you* want to hear, such as politicians or salesmen.

If you tell a lie as an adult, will being confronted bring out the "truth"? Not likely. You will probably become ever more desperate to tell your questioner what he or she wants to hear. When you lie, you are **behaving as** a frightened *four-year-old* who doesn't want to risk disapproval, who isn't interested in the consequences three weeks or three years from now. You will say whatever you think Mother or Father or Auntie or Grandpa expects you to say just to gain their approval and thereby survive the moment. Telling the truth may hurt, but it especially hurts the adult with this *four-year-old* hang-up.

If, on the other hand, you were allowed as a child to tell the truth without being scolded, punished, or rejected by the grown-ups in your life, your self-image was secure enough at age four to express your true thoughts without fear. As an adult, you will continue to tell the truth, whether or not others approve; indeed, if you fear the disapproval of others, you cannot be true to yourself.

## SUPPRESSED EMOTIONAL EXPRESSION: BED WETTING

Bed wetting is normal and expected for an infant, but when it continues beyond the age of four, there is a personality arrest at work.

During directed age reenactment, it became clear that adult patients who had wet their beds past the age of four shared a common pattern. Although, as young children, they had good imaginations and a full range of emotional energies, they weren't allowed—especially *around the age of four*—to express their feelings. Anger and crying were not acceptable, nor were exuberance and enthusiasm. One of the only ways these children could express themselves was in dreams. Only then could they let their tension go, could they feel free to do their own thing—with the result that they also wet their beds.

Now, when I work with parents whose children are bed wetters, I encourage them to let their children have more freedom to express all of their emotions; as the parents learn to relax restrictions on their children, the symptom of bed wetting clears up.

## LEARNING DISABILITY: STUPIDITY AS A DEFENSE

You are born with an enormous amount of intuitive knowledge. During the first six years of life, if you feel safe and are encouraged, you can bring this forward to your consciousness. On the other hand, if your life is structured and highly controlled, little of this intuitive knowledge will become available to you after the age of six. From then on, you only accumulate information and learn how to apply techniques. What many call "stupidity," and some call "learning disability," is actually confusion that can be traced to a four-year-old hang-up.

When you are four years old, you often ask a second question before your first one can be answered. When your parents get upset at this, you feel rejected and fearful; if this occurs often enough, you feel insecure, afraid to ask any questions. So later, when you attend nursery school you are even afraid to ask directions to go to the bathroom. To protect yourself from your fear of rejection, you form the *four-year-old* personality arrest of "stupidity." By not asking questions, you go through life appearing to be stupid simply because you don't want to risk rejection. Your not asking questions leads naturally to confusion, which adds to your "disability" to learn even though you are perfectly capable of learning.

When your parents tell you something, you immediately accept it as a fact, that is, unless you are aware of some obvious contradicting evidence in your immediate surroundings. All is well and good until one parent says something that contradicts what the other said. One statement must be true —and therefore the other one must be false, maybe even dangerous. Without asking questions, you have no easy way to sort things out. Now if you are introduced to conflicting views, from older siblings, other relatives, playmates at nursery, friends of the family, your confusion intensifies. You are so busy trying to sort out what is true from what is false that your learning becomes stalled. If, as a four-year-old, you are bombarded with conflicting information such as continual family arguments, you learn to block out *all* information by appearing hopelessly stupid. This *four-year-old* personality arrest is greatly aggravated when your parents force you to repudiate the information you have gathered by yourself.

Say your mother takes you to a doctor's appointment and the doctor does not see you until an hour later. When the doctor gives a perfunctory apology, Mother says, "That's all right, we don't mind." Mother's response is devastating to your sense of self, because everything you perceived about your mother indicated she was greatly annoyed, upset, and angry because the doctor was so late. Now, in an indirect suggestion, she tells you that what you perceived so clearly is false.

Indirect suggestion is far more powerful and effective than direct statements. If a parent tells you that you are stupid, it hurts you and you become defensive. But this is only a fraction as hurtful as when the same parent tells your neighbor about the "stupid" things you do—and you overhear. In the first instance, you may be able to deny and defend yourself against the attack, but in the second, you believe it must be true, and you accept the label "stupid" as fact.

## IMPOTENCE

If, faced with repeated rebuffs and criticism, a boy around the age of four feels everything he does is short of his parents' expected standards, he may no longer try to reach those standards, or if he does try, he assumes he will fail. He learns to fail *in advance* as a defense against disappointing his parents. As an adult, when under the stress of having to perform, this *four-year-old* personality arrest can manifest itself as impotence. Men with chronic impotence typically suffer from a **compound personality arrest**, combining their *four-year-old* fear of failure with the much earlier personality arrest of poor body image—formed usually *around the age of one*—which limits their ability to have intimate relationships.

## LAZINESS, PROCRASTINATION

How many lazy two-year-olds have you seen? At two, you look into everything and try everything. You are up early and you are running from morning to night, except for those periods when Mother puts you down for a nap.

At four, you earnestly desire to help out in all the household and family activities. But if your parents don't take the time or have the patience necessary to teach you what to do and how, if instead they criticize and demean your bumbling efforts, you become fearful of their rejection. Nothing you do seems to be right. Worse, you face almost certain rejection if you try to do things on your own or in your own way.

What your parents are teaching you is fear. You learn that you are safer if you do nothing, if you are "lazy." All of us have received "lessons" in laziness. The most indolent people are those who have been subjected to repeated, forceful suggestions of inadequacy as four-year-olds.

Laziness equals fear of "doing it wrong." No adult is really comfortable being lazy, but you can become permanently labeled "lazy" if, as a *four-year-old*, you are repeatedly humiliated with comparisons, called names, and shamed for your bumbling efforts to perform as an equal member of the family.

Suppose, at four, you want to be helpful and decide to wash Dad's new car. You know "how to do it" because you have seen Dad with a bucket and soapy water swabbing the car. So early Sunday morning when Dad is still in bed, you gather your supplies, a bucket of water, an old rag, and a box of laundry soap. You dab and scrub the parts of the vehicle you can reach until you are tired. You are proud of your achievement. After coffee, Dad sees his new car and becomes livid with rage. He not only spanks and scolds you but, by dismissing your effort, he *rejects* you as an incompetent person.

What happens to your self-image? How soon will you volunteer again?

Procrastination, another *four-year-old* defense, is the act of someone who believes that taking the initiative to do something will most likely result in criticism and rejection. As a procrastinator, you don't rush into any project because you don't want to rush into disaster. Have you ever heard someone say, "Boy, you'd think it would kill you to fix up this house." It is less a joke than that person imagines.

Related to procrastination is the lack of drive to complete or follow through on a task, project, or program. You start out with great interest and enthusiasm, but along the way, often when you are almost there, you begin to feel intimidated. You make rationalizations to relieve yourself of the burden of completion. Perhaps you are someone who got through most of a course, say, and then dropped out, even though you could have finished it successfully. Nothing anyone could do or say would entice you to resume and finish the course.

Inability to achieve goals or complete tasks is a fairly common problem, and most of the people I have encountered with it have had a similar background. Although also established at a *four-year-old* level, this personality arrest often doesn't become evident until the teenage or adult years. You enroll at a college or trade school, you are enthusiastic and eager, but along the way, you rationalize why you should not continue. You drop out, only to start again in some other area. This pattern is repeated throughout your lifetime. Not reaching goals or finishing projects is a defense mechanism, implanted in your subconscious mind at the age of four, to protect you from rejection when what you did was never "good enough."

## INAPPROPRIATE SMILE AND LAUGHTER

An adult who smiles repeatedly for no reason while talking (former President Jimmy Carter, for instance) or who laughs repeatedly when there is no humor in what is said is **behaving as** a *four-year-old* afraid of being criticized or rejected.

At four, you want to let your own thoughts or views flow freely, but you learn, after repeated rebuffs that this isn't acceptable. To avoid criticism, you must tell the grown-ups in your life only what they want to hear—*unless* you couch your views in smiles and laughter. You learn that false humor and contrived smiles allow you to express thoughts that would otherwise be rejected.

Repeatedly criticizing children for what they think or feel represents a form of thought control. When a child is *four years old,* this leads to the personality arrest of inappropriate smile and laughter.

## STAMMERING

Speech starts spontaneously in growing children. Once their nervous system is adequately developed, they have increasing voluntary control over their lips, tongue, larynx, and vocal cords, and they start imitating the sounds of the people in their immediate surroundings.

Speech develops in children naturally—without the urging and cajoling of their parents. By the time you are three years old, you are babbling on and on without expending any great effort or thinking about what you are saying or how you are pronouncing your words. It is almost an automatic response.

If, however, when you are *four years old,* you have anxious parents who correct your every word or your pronunciation, then in fear of rejection, your speech will change from spontaneous to hesitatingly calculated. You will think consciously of each syllable you speak. You will pay utmost attention to how you pronounce each word, rather than to expressing your thoughts. This fear of having your speech corrected makes you so anxious you learn to stammer, and if your anxiety is not alleviated, you may stammer throughout your life.

## AGE FIVE

At five, if your emotional development hasn't been blocked by personality arrests, you have a strong sense of identity. Free from residual anger, you begin to develop a sense of humor. You are imaginative, enthusiastic, and inventive; you can express your own thoughts, and you can see that the rules can be interpreted in many ways. Your growing broadmindedness needs to be tempered by a set of strong personal values and philosophy of life, or you may become permissive or self-indulgent. You learn to associate and compete.

## COMPETITIVENESS

At five you are beginning to relate to others your own age in nursery school, kindergarten, swim class, and elsewhere. You play in groups and make friends and rivals. You want and demand recognition. You stay focused in what you are doing from one day to the next. With friendly competition, you can stay focused even longer and be stimulated to do better.

If, on the other hand, you are *forced* to compete, based on what you *do* rather than who you *are*, if you are forced to achieve goals set for you by others, regardless of your own feelings, wishes, or preferences, and if, further, others (especially your family) insist you must best everyone else, no matter what, then to protect yourself you may form the *five-year-old* personality arrest of competitiveness.

In this country, business and finance place a premium on healthy competition and getting ahead. *Defensive* competitiveness, however, is anything but healthy; it promotes dishonesty, cheating, and even cruelty, as winning becomes everything, and when it crosses over from the business world, it can destroy intimacy and family life.

## CRITICISM

Unlike genuine help or suggestions, there is no such thing as "constructive criticism." Criticism—however qualified—always means putting someone down, asserting the critic's superiority over the criticized.

At four, when you are criticized, put down for anything and everything you do, you become wounded and hurt. By five, you learn that when your parents and older siblings are criticizing you, they are also dominating you, that they can frighten and control you just with a stern look. Whenever you are made to feel inadequate and inferior, you learn to defend yourself by putting your younger siblings or playmates down—by dominating *them*. You form the *five-year-old* personality arrest of criticism.

Later in life, when you feel inadequate or fearful of competition, you criticize or put other people down—your employees, your younger associates or friends, and especially your children. You **behave as** a frightened *five-year-old*, defending yourself against your fear of inadequacy by dominating others.

## DOGMATISM

Suppose, for the first four years of your life, you had a low self-image—you felt that no one accepted or approved of you for what you were. At five, you make a wonderful discovery. There is a system of rules and if you follow these rules, your family, teachers, and even strangers suddenly start approving of you. You can become a little dictator by shaping up your younger brothers and sisters, by making them follow the rules, too.

The more rigidly you follow the rules—the more dogmatic you are—the more your rigid mother or dictatorial father seems to approve of you. In reality, of course, they don't accept you for who you *are*, but for what you *do*. They and the other adults in your life approve of you because you have learned to do the "right" thing in the "right" way, and even then, they approve of you only as long as you can *keep* doing it.

The *five-year-old* personality arrest of dogmatism is most commonly found in firstborn children. Parents have and dedicate more time to structure the behavior of their firstborn. Most middle children are taught simply by example, which often makes of them better-adjusted individuals. In general, the less effective you feel as a person, the more you need that sense of power over others through rigid rules and force. The most common "cure" for doubt or indecision is the rigid rule, which gives a ready answer for everything. It requires no thought at all, just remembering "the right thing."

A clear example of socially functional dogmatism is the Marine drill sergeant. The sense of discipline and esprit de corps he can instill in his recruits may well save their lives in combat, where irresolution and indecisiveness can be fatal. Problems arise, however, if the drill sergeant fails to separate his dogmatic professional behavior from his social and family life.

The pursuit of power has been a far more driving ambition than the pursuit of wealth or love. If you study the lives of famous despots throughout history, you will find that they all had the personality arrest of dogmatic *five-year-old* children whose own rules were the most important drive in their lives. Stalin was perhaps the greatest of all five-year-old despots. He feared and put to death all who questioned his dogma or threatened his power.

With this personality arrest you fear those who believe in their own intrinsic worth, who are independent, who think and decide for themselves. Dogmatic rules and regulation at home, in school, in the church or state reflect leaders' lack of faith in themselves as well as in others. Those who demand blind obedience to dogmatic ideologies or creeds have little regard, much less respect, for the uniqueness of any single individual, including themselves.

## BIGOTRY, HATRED, AND VENGEFULNESS

As a child responding to repeated, prolonged threats, you may combine or convert earlier emotional defenses (personality arrests) to form new and generally more resistant defenses. The *five-year-old* defenses of bigotry and vengefulness are compound personality arrests: bigotry combines two *three-year-old* defenses, bitterness and resentment and blind obedience, while vengefulness combines two *five-year-old* defenses, hatred and dogmatism. Hatred, by contrast, is a **converted personality arrest**, formed by converting (*at age five*) the infantile defense of violent temper (*birth to age one*).

As a *three-year-old* growing up in a hostile, dysfunctional household—and angry at not being acknowledged or accepted—you learn to protect yourself from the pain of repeated rejection by becoming bitter and resentful. When that fails to gain you what you need, you "get along" with your parents and older siblings by learning the defense of blind obedience. Day in and day out, you hear what your mother or father, your older brothers or sisters say about groups of people they consider inferior (on whatever grounds); day in and day out, you see how they behave and you feel how they feel toward these outsiders. At *five*, still unacknowledged and unaccepted, and still looking to your parents and older siblings for validation, you follow their example. You form the *five-year-old* compound personality arrest of bigotry.

Suppose instead that *shortly after you are born*, in response to repeated threats of rejection around you, you turn your infantile rage into the personality arrest of violent temper. By the age of five, your critical reasoning can clearly focus on the person, thing, or situation you identify as the source of rejection. If at five you still feel rejected time after time, then, following your parents' example or acting on your own, you protect yourself against this rejection by turning your violent temper into the *five-year-old* converted personality arrest of hatred. Each encounter with the source of your rejection—or with its image—re-ignites and reinforces your hatred. Like bigotry, hatred is based on anger; unlike bigotry, which is a group defense, held and passed on by one group and directed toward another, hatred is intensely *personal*.

And finally suppose, as a *five-year-old* child, you have learned to hate. Finding yourself repeatedly blocked in your self-expression, and repeatedly punished or rejected for any solutions or ideas of your own, you learn that, by rigidly conforming to the rules—and as long as you do—you are approved of. You want to keep the status quo. You feel safe only within this conformity. When the rules are broken—and your safety therefore threatened—you want the offender punished. "An eye for an eye, a tooth for a tooth" is justice at a five-year-old level. You combine the *five-year-old* defenses of hatred and dogmatism to form the compound personality arrest of vengefulness. If you can contain your vengefulness within socially approved limits, you are a good candidate for the military service or law enforcement.

Television and movies do much to glorify and legitimize adults **behaving as** dogmatic, vengeful *five-year-olds*, often implying that, as an officer of the law, for example, you are perfectly justified in violating the rights of other human beings—and in depriving them of their lives if need be. Retaliation and revenge are outstanding TV themes. Getting even seems to be the American way (the five-year-old way)—it is always "somebody else's fault."

As with hatred, the excuses used to rationalize revenge serve to "justify" unconscionable acts. But these excuses are merely constructs of the conscious mind. **Behaving as** a threatened, angry, vengeful five-year-old, you strike your supposed enemy before he or she can further damage you. Your "explanation" is a rationalization after the fact.

## THE DREAMER: FANTASY VERSUS IMAGINATION

Repeated failure to achieve unrealistic goals is a *five-year-old* hang-up. At two, you had the basic drive to assert your individuality. You wanted to do everything your own way even though you knew little about how to accomplish it. Now at five, you want to do everything because you believe you have all the answers.

Suppose your parents, afraid you might get hurt, protect you by doing all the harder and riskier tasks for you in your first four years, thus depriving you of the benefit of learning on your own. Instead, you learn by proxy, from a distance, without the hands-on, detailed experience you need to complete a project. Never able to learn from your mistakes and failures, you become a perennial five-year-old, a dreamer, and later in life, often a business failure.

Suppose you are finally given the chance to fix something or undertake a project by yourself and you fail. You quickly become disillusioned with this firsthand experience, and you resort to rationalization to explain the failure. Through **fantasy**, you construct a scheme to do anything—without the need of having a real foundation.

Here we need to contrast **imagination** and **fantasy**. **Imagination** is one of your most valuable assets. When you imagine something you want to do, your conscious mind combines real images, complete feelings or pictures that come from your subconscious mind (perhaps from the universal mind). Carefully filling in the details based on everything you have learned, felt, or experienced to that time—and everything you intuitively *know* to be true—it then assesses the feasibility of what you imagine. **Fantasy**, on the other hand, is your conscious mind's attempt to *synthesize* something you want to do. Each step of your fantasy involves wishful thinking, the conscious combination of *un*real (incomplete, unexperienced) images, entirely apart from what you have learned, felt, or experienced—or intuitively *know* to be true—with no effort to assess or evaluate what you fantasize. Fantasy is similar to rationalization, allowing you to find any excuse or extenuating circumstance to convince yourself and others of the validity of what you fantasize.

If, unlike the dreamer, you learned through trial and error as an infant and child, your conscious mind is free to view projects and undertakings objectively, to ferret out any problems, to *imagine* solutions, and to weigh the costs and relative merits of those solutions.

## SUMMARY

As a developing child between the ages of two and a half and six, you respond to pressure from your parents, peers, and society by accommodating and adjusting to others. If this pressure is excessive, unreasonable, or premature, you feel put upon or threatened. You protect yourself by forming **emotional defenses** (**personality arrests**), which, unless recognized and released, will determine your behavior from then on.

Rooted in your attitude and relationship to others and to society, the personality arrests of **childhood** range from anxiety, guilt, **depression**, and blind obedience to aggressiveness, duplicity, pretentiousness, and dogmatism; from **passive aggressiveness**, conformism, indecisiveness, and bigotry to perfectionism, competitiveness, criticism, and vengefulness.

Whether formed in childhood or **infancy**, your personality arrests stunt and distort your **self-image**, which is all but completely set by the time you are six—and which, as chapter 5 explains, will govern how you relate to others for the rest of your life.

# 5

# Your Self-Image and How You Relate to Others

Relationships—the ways we become comfortable with and emotionally close to another person—are the most important things in our lives, as popular songs, stories, and movies overwhelmingly attest.

In most instances, the bar to closer relationships is fear of intimacy—fear you were taught as an infant or child and which your subconscious mind calls up to protect you from rejection, abandonment, and death. The less emotionally developed your self-image is, the more vulnerable you will feel—and the greater your fear of intimacy.

Almost all of us come into this world as warm, loving, open beings. As we are taught fears and anger—and form defenses (personality arrests)—our natural evolution becomes blocked and harder and harder to fulfill.

## CHOICES

As an experienced therapist, I have learned that patients, including children, waste their time and mine when they attempt to explain or defend their positions. I will listen and encourage all questions and new ideas—but not rationalizations (justifications). Unless the dialogue can be changed to one that isn't threatening to the patient, I close the interview. Basically, there is only one reason that you do anything, and that is because you *choose* to do it—because you *want* to do it. Any other explanation is a fabrication after the fact.

This is a very fundamental concept, which divides people into two different groups: (1) those who are victims; and (2) those who are their own persons and can choose to direct their own lives.

Life is composed of a continuous string of choices.

Suppose it's Sunday. You can go to church with your mother, although you have no interest in the service, or you can remain at home and later be subjected to the disapproval of your mother (who happens to be domineering). The service only lasts for an hour, while your mother's anger could last all day. So you choose the "lesser evil."

Or suppose you ask your four-year-old daughter, "Why did you eat the cookie?" She doesn't dare say, "Because I wanted it." She knows you would disapprove and might even punish her. So she searches for an answer that will placate you—she chooses to tell a lie instead of the truth.

As a prison doctor, I used to explain to each of my patients that we were both volunteers. Each of us had to take some action to bring us to the same place. I applied for the position of prison doctor, and my patient put himself in prison by engaging in a crime or choosing to be with someone who was committing a crime. I might complain that my patients are argumentative and unappreciative; my patient might complain that prison life is hard and the guards intolerant, but we both volunteered—chose—to be in our current situation.

When you can own up to the fact that you chose an action for every situation that contributed to your present state, you can then begin to take control of the direction of the rest of your life. As long as you see yourself as a victim, there is no hope because you will never be able to direct your own life.

It may seem that, of the choices available to you, none of them is satisfactory, but you still *have* choices, and that enables you to direct your life.

## TRUTH

Your actions and reactions are based upon what you believe to be true. You don't want to be an undesirable person, so why is it that you sometimes act directly opposite to your best interests? Telling yourself to be "this way or that" may be fun and interesting to do, but it is all at a conscious—superficial—level. To effect a change in your feelings, you must reach the deepest level of your subconscious mind. Simply trying to force yourself to change is not only useless, it is counterproductive.

Truth is a very personal concept. If we all believed in the same truth, our emotional reactions would be the same. Truth is also the most variable of concepts. We all learn from different sets of information, and our emotional truths are completely and uniquely subjective.

If you believe something to be true, then you feel and react with confidence on the basis of that premise. Reflect on your teenage years. Would you want to be held to all the beliefs you had at that time? Your current truth is based on the information that you have now. Most of your conclusions are sound, and it is necessary for you to hold on to them. Santa Claus is a pleasing **image (fantasy)** for an infant or young child, but as you get added information, your image of Santa shifts. Your images of Columbus, General Custer, and the heroes of the Indian Wars have undoubtedly changed since you first entered school. All truths and images change as you get more information upon which to draw revised conclusions. Images are essential to understanding your feelings, your prejudices, and your defenses. Only by reviewing and studying the past, how your images were formed and how they changed, can you understand how you came to be who you are. Never attack other people's "truth." For them, it is not simply a truth, it is *the* truth.

## NO ABNORMAL BEHAVIOR

Barring mental disorders caused by brain damage, dementia, and psychosis, there is no such thing as "abnormal" human behavior. In every other instance, you can locate the place, time, and event in infancy or early childhood when behavior, unacceptable in an older child or adult, would be entirely normal and appropriate for an infant or child.

Some years ago, it was reported that, during criminal trials, laypersons using their intuition scored as well as a panel of psychiatrists in distinguishing the insane from the sane. If you observe how others behave—*without* judgment or explanation—you can instinctively distinguish behavior that is infantile or childish (evidence of personality arrest) from behavior that is "out of it," disconnected from reality (evidence of mental disorder).

You will never have complete information about the circumstances, pressures, and fears that motivate others; therefore, you should neither judge nor excuse them. But—so long as you *refrain* from explaining or excusing their behavior—your observations and conclusions are valid. If these others are **behaving as** two-year-olds, that is the limit of their emotional development in that particular area of their lives. When under stress, that is the best you can expect them ever to behave.

When you aren't under stress, you can pretend to **act like** an adult, a professional, or a parent. You are an actor when you want to impress, provided you aren't hassled. The real, basic you can only be seen when you are under stress. If you are totally evolved in all areas of your life, you will **behave as** an adult under all circumstances.

How many times have you observed how childish some people become when they have a little pain or sickness? How often have you witnessed people under the influence of drugs or alcohol **behave as** inconsiderate infants or children with total disregard for those around them? If before marriage, you observe your fiancé abuse himself with alcohol, his pretense at being mature will be wiped away by the alcohol. He is **behaving as** an "unworthy" child or "worthless" infant. What you see is the best you can hope for each time he finds himself under stress, now and for the next fifty years. Believe what you see—make no excuses for anyone, including yourself. Any time you make excuses, you become part of the problem. An emotionally mature person after overindulging in alcohol will simply fall asleep, with no perceptible change in personality.

## NEEDS VERSUS WANTS

In general, you tend to get what you want while your needs go unfulfilled. Just as we have divided conscious from subconscious drives, we can divide **needs** from **wants**.

At a conscious level, you have **wants**—you can create a daydream or fantasy of what you want, what you think will be desirable for you. If you only had that new car or that special person for a partner, then you would feel good or happy. Getting that new car or special partner may give you momentary satisfaction, but it doesn't—in and of itself—create any lasting or convincing feeling that you have grown or developed, or that you have enlarged your awareness of the world you live in.

At a subconscious level, on the other hand, you have **needs** for fulfillment. When you grow or achieve intimacy with another person, you experience fulfillment that lasts. When you learn to play the piano, your life has an added dimension.

## WORSHIP

From the beginning of time we have been worshippers. The history of all peoples everywhere tells us of men and women bowing in adoration of somebody or something they felt was greater than they.

Most people, whether they are religious or agnostic, have the need to hold in veneration some force that controls their destinies for good or evil. Ironically, some very devout Christians hold the devil in the greatest awe, and the vehemence of their denunciations makes the devil a power of the first order in their lives.

Which brings us to the heart of the problem.

Worship is basically a system, whether public or private, of ranking an object, force, or deity *above* the worshipper. But every time you elevate someone or something, you necessarily degrade yourself. When you worship a supreme, almighty, all-knowing deity, a deity that manages and controls everything, you at the same time accept that you have no force or power. You make yourself a helpless and irresponsible child. It follows that whatever happens is going to happen; you can do nothing about it—and you are *not* responsible. You **behave as** a *six-week-old infant* totally at the mercy of your parents.

To worship is to escape from taking your rightful place in shaping your destiny. Obviously, when there is someone or something in charge of everything, you are no longer expected to be in charge of yourself.

Reverence without worshipping in no way negates the concept of a supreme force in the universe. Quite the contrary, it *affirms* it. If you, as a member of the human race, believe you have a soul or at least some spark of spirit in common with all other humans from all times; further, if you consider that this spark is part of the supreme force in our universe and that all of the parts of this force seek recombination and unity as the ultimate goal, then it follows that no other person is greater than you, for the same supreme force is within both of you. It also follows that you cannot be above or below the supreme force because you are part of that force, and it is part of you—you are one.

To worship is to make your God small and vindictive—to expect favor and punishment, not for who you *are* but for what you *do*. You cannot be free if you worship anything or anybody.

## LOVE

**Love** is said to be the most important emotion of man.

The dictionary gives the word "love" a long list of definitions, which in itself implies there is much vagueness in meaning. As I see it, by "love" our society means something like this: the active energy you voluntarily or involuntarily put forth toward another person for your own benefit and satisfaction in the hope that the other person will appreciate and return it to you according to your expectations. Our dysfunctional society has fashioned this concept of love out of an apparent, desperate need for *approval*: the one who "loves" expects, indeed demands, approval from the "loved."

From working with hundreds of patients, I found that what we truly need is **acceptance**, not approval. Our basic human need is to be accepted simply for being who we are. When by the age of two and a half, you feel you haven't been *accepted* for who you *are*, you lower your expectations and simply seek to be *approved of* for what you *do*. You are taught, both at home and in church, that if you do the "right thing," you will be approved of ("accepted") and therefore loved. In reality, as soon as you fail to do as you are expected, you will be spurned—by your parents, your family, your group. What we universally desire is the acceptance accorded newborn infants, who are taken home before they have had the opportunity to prove themselves in any way.

The difference between acceptance and "love" (as it is popularly understood) is the difference between being wanted for simply *being* and being wanted for *doing*.

In its true, enduring sense, love is entirely passive, something automatic—you cannot *prevent* yourself from loving someone who accepts you for who you *are*. You can receive and have as much love as you want, for if you truly accept a man, a woman, a baby, a child, that individual will *automatically* love you and will want to be around you. This is a universal, automatic, natural human reaction.

We go where we feel at least some acceptance. Teenagers who feel little or no acceptance at home join gangs, where they are less criticized and feel at least some degree of equality, closeness, and acceptance.

There are individuals whose self-image is so low that they will run away from full and open acceptance—they feel they are unworthy. The only way to reach them is by slowly and patiently creating an environment where they can feel safe. It will take time and patience for them to trust you enough to come near. Only when these individuals feel safe can you approach them and will they allow themselves to be accepted and loved.

## GROUPS

We learned millions of years ago that we couldn't survive as isolated individuals. A social structure is an absolute necessity for orderly coexistence. To belong to a group, an organization, or an institution, you must surrender some autonomy and abide by many of that group's rules or creeds.

If you are a mature adult, you can go along with the group by temporarily forgoing some of your prerogatives. If the group becomes too oppressive, you voluntarily withdraw from it.

If, on the other hand, you have little self-confidence, you may rigidly adhere to positions of the group, be it club, team, church, political party, or religious cult. Doing this, you again assume the status of a dependent child, avoiding responsibility as you bypass your own perceptions in favor of the group's rules.

When someone asks you to describe your group or organization and you find yourself defending or rationalizing your membership, you are **behaving as** a fearful *four-year-old* who feels compelled to make up excuses for his or her actions. If you react even more strongly to neutral questions, as though they were personal attacks, you are **behaving as** a frightened *three-year-old* whose need to belong and be recognized was denied as a child and who must therefore identify all the more strongly—rigidly—with his or her group as an adult.

In the Nuremberg trials after World War II and in the My Lai massacre trial during the Vietnam War, the courts rejected the excuse of "just following orders" and upheld the conclusion that individuals are responsible for their actions.

Institutions, whether they are church, state, or social institutions, are designed to perpetuate themselves, and as a consequence they have no regard for the individual. Divergence from the "party line" will result in exclusion. A teenager who chooses to wear neat and well-fitting clothes may be shunned by his classmates, a gang member who chooses to earn good grades may be ousted by her gang, a parishioner who chooses to divorce and remarry may be excommunicated by his church, and a member who marries someone of another race may be excluded by her social club. Belonging is necessary for the social order to exist—surrendering your identity, or your basic values, to that order is not. The compulsion to surrender to the will of the group is a childish defense (personality arrest) formed *around the age of three*.

## MARRIAGE

More than any other institution, marriage has suffered from the ill effects of *unrealistic expectations*. For all the progress we have made in the areas of science and technology, our ability to understand one another realistically and objectively seems to have regressed.

The most devastating words two people considering marriage can say to each other are "I love you because I need you" and "You make me happy and you will for the rest of my life." This expectation is not only unreasonable, it is impossible. The perfect person has not been discovered and if there is one, he or she could not find an adequate mate. Placing unrealistic expectations upon your partner is the beginning of the end for many, if not most, marriages.

We all have our hang-ups and our faults. Typically, both persons in courtship make excuses for their partner's hang-ups (personality arrests) and faults even when these are obvious to everyone. Common excuses are "Oh, you're judging him too harshly" or "She'll be okay as soon as she gets away from her family" or "I'll help him get over this problem" or "That might be true for another man, but I can handle her." Later, the hang-up you most excuse in your partner proves to be the very one that most irritates you.

You can best use your intuitive powers in the initial phase of courtship. At the first meeting, you immediately sense the potential in your partner. Although you can accurately appraise the potential in others, you may have trouble consciously identifying the potential within yourself. You may have been taught all of your life to play down your talents and to control or hide your feelings, with the result that you underestimate your worth.

After you have seen the potential that attracts you to your partner, the second phase of courtship begins. As you get to know one another, the intuitive powers of your subconscious mind let you judge whether your partner has the same degree of emotional maturity that you have. If your partner is much more mature or emotionally evolved in all significant respects, then you will feel uncomfortable and inadequate in his or her presence. On the other hand, if your partner behaves more childishly than you, you will also feel uncomfortable—and put off. In order to be comfortable, you must find someone who is at the same level of emotional maturity as you are.

In all human relationships we play-act; we pretend to be more adult, more mature than we actually feel. Most of the time, we carry this off—especially during courtship because we want to favorably impress our partners. This charade falls away when stress and tension return us to our basic (infantile or childish) selves.

On a subconscious level, you are as much aware of your hang-ups as you are of any defect in your body. Your subconscious awareness allows you to read other people and instinctively to know their personality arrests, just as it tells you—automatically and subconsciously—where one hand is in relation to the other, or whether you are moving or standing, or how fast you are walking. You can bring this subconscious awareness to your conscious attention, even though ordinarily it doesn't occupy your conscious mind.

The third phase of courtship, realistic selection of a mate, involves identifying your partner's specific hang-ups (personality arrests). You almost invariably will seek someone who complements you by supplying socially acceptable strengths in areas where you consider yourself weak.

It is commonly said that you marry someone who is like your mother or father—or both. There is an underlying emotional determinant to this conventional wisdom. For example, the woman who has only known parental domination considers herself incapable of making her own decisions. Accordingly, she seeks as husband a man who appears to take charge, who dominates those around him.

On the surface, this looks like a workable combination, and for a while, it is. Eventually, however, the combination can only lead to discontent. Subconsciously, the wife resents her husband's putdowns. She may loathe or even hate the parent who treated her in such a patronizing manner; she will in turn learn to hate her husband, who is treating her in the same childish fashion. She is not, at heart, a weak or indecisive person, but she learned, as an infant or child, to play this demeaning role to save her life.

The overbearing or manipulating man, in turn, will seek out a subservient woman as wife, so that he can continue the charade that he is the only one who is important. At a deeper level, however, he will have little respect for anyone he can push around. Although these two types could live together fairly well before marriage and for a short time after, each one will come to have less and less respect for the other. Neither of these roles fosters understanding or acceptance.

This hypothetical marriage will run into great trouble if one of the partners begins to mature emotionally; especially if the subservient wife matures emotionally from the little, three-year-old girl to a full-grown woman making adult choices. Unless the husband also matures at the same time, unless he is able to give up his five-year-old dictatorial attitude, the marriage cannot succeed. At best, the two will be hostile roommates.

A marriage can be held together because of financial problems, children, guilt, church affiliations, or fear of the unknown, but unless some intimacy through mutual acceptance develops, the relationship will never be a happy one.

After the infatuation recedes and the fantasies fade, a married couple needs true intimacy—where each partner understands, accepts, and responds to the other—to keep love alive. Intimacy can occur only when partners shut down their conscious appraisal of what they are saying or doing (forget about themselves) long enough to concentrate on what the other person is feeling.

As both partners feel understood and accepted, they can be themselves without any pretenses. They can accept, understand, and respond to each other as they *are*. This intimate understanding is only possible when they let down their defenses, at least for a while.

You have no "rights" over any other person, especially not over your spouse, for in truth no one wants to be owned—or controlled.

In marriage you need to provide your partner safe space. You owe each other nothing but *acceptance*. If you feel enough "good" in yourself, you will feel worthy of the acceptance.

When marriage partners can be together and become comfortable with each other, when they can mutually accept and enjoy the whole idea of the other—without trying to change or do away with any part of the other—they each have a greater chance of fulfilling their own potentials, thus assuring the happiness and fulfillment of both.

Your marriage is working when you, with the tacit acknowledgment and encouragement of your spouse, attempt projects or relationships you would not possibly attempt on your own.

There is no perfect union—only an unsurpassed, mutual accommodation.

## DIVORCE

Divorce is a remedy for two people who are uncomfortable with one another. The root cause of almost all divorces is fantasy. One partner falls in love with the other, not as that person truly *is* in real life, but rather with the *fantasy* of what the other could be if all his or her potentials were fully developed. As long as the illusion is kept actively alive, the marriage is kept in a state of honeymoon. When the unrealistic expectations aren't fulfilled, interest in the union falters.

Consider, for the sake of comparison, the situation of a young boy and a young girl who meet in a playground. If the children are the same age and size, they play together or fight together more or less as equals. But what if the girl, say, is eight and the boy only four, as sometimes happens? The older child has to gear her activities down to the level of her four-year-old playmate, who in turn must try his best to keep up with her, especially when she runs or throws him the ball. They play together well, for a while at least, but if forced to stay together for any extended period of time, each will feel uncomfortable, until they decide to part company—divorce.

Now consider a marriage where the partners are different in their degree of emotional maturity. Just as the older child in our comparison eventually grew tired of playing at the level of her younger playmate—and he of trying to play at her older level—so each of our marriage partners eventually tires of functioning at the other's lower or higher emotional level in order to communicate or have any kind of relationship.

Problems arise in marriages because we expect everybody to grow emotionally, but most people stop maturing before the age of six. If they do nothing to allow themselves to grow

—to release their personality arrests—they will remain the same for the rest of their lives.

When you married, you sought and found, say, a kindred four-year-old. You were blissfully happy when the two of you played the games that all four-year-olds love to play. Difficulties arose when only one of you grew emotionally, and the maturing spouse wanted to upgrade the games.

Suddenly, that spouse can no longer stand the other's childish behavior. No matter how much counseling and outside help you may seek and use, there can never be parity, unless the other person also allows for emotional growth. The only good solution is to upgrade your ability to participate with enjoyment in games at the same age level, and if this does not happen, eventually one or both of you will develop the urge to seek a new playmate.

When you are married and continue to live with a spouse who under stress reverts to an infantile or childish behavior (personality arrest), expect your spouse to behave and compete at the same level as your own infants or children. Later, as your children mature, they will simply ignore their father or mother; they no longer want to play infantile or childish games.

As a rule, with few exceptions, the partner who grows emotionally is the one who wants to get away (divorce) from the partner who cannot overcome his or her personality arrest. The emotionally younger partner will in childish fashion try to hold on to the more mature partner and will most likely seek sympathy out of the feeling that he or she is being abandoned.

Marriage and rearing children are a business like running a farm or growing grapes, except that your product is a healthy, well-adjusted group of people. Affection is a necessary ingredient, but it isn't likely to flourish when all the family members **behave as** infants or children, acting out their infantile or childish hang-ups to control the other members of the family. You can certainly have affection for babies and little children, but you cannot conduct business with them as equal partners.

A perfect marriage is one where both partners grow at an equal pace as the couple goes through life. If the partners mature at an equal rate but in separate directions, they may mutually agree to divorce, but they will remain staunch friends for the rest of their lives.

## TEENAGE GANGS

Your most driving need is to be accepted. Acceptance is seldom, if ever, complete but you will take all you can get (to the degree that you feel worthy of it). You will be drawn to that partner, group, or gang where you feel most comfortable. When teenagers feel ill at ease at home, they will seek association with those who they perceive are more open to them. That doesn't mean their parents don't love them or have their best interests in mind; it's just that the teenagers' perceptions are different.

When, as an adolescent, you have largely given up trying to be accepted for what you *are*, you will turn your attention to gaining approval for what you *do*. You can find approval for your rebellious behavior in your teenage group (or gang) who share your feelings.

The basis for this rebellious attitude is a two-year-old personality arrest. Suppose, as an investigative infant between two and two and a half, you were thwarted in much of your explorations by overprotective or disapproving parents. You found when you tried to assert your individuality, you weren't accepted. So you learned to delay this necessary expression of self-assertiveness. By the age of twelve to fourteen, you have grown physically and you get a kick of energy from your erupting sex hormones. You feel that the time has come for you to be an independent individual rather than a controlled infant.

You, who were such a seemingly meek and conforming child from age three to thirteen, now become blatant in asserting your independence. This is a tremendous shock to your parents, who for ten years have suppressed your self-assertiveness, who have molded you to conform to their own ideas of what a child should be. There is no way for you to skip this normal stage of emotional maturation. When the stage is delayed for ten or eleven years, the results can be devastating. As a two-year-old, you were fairly harmless in spilling, messing, climbing, and breaking, but when you delay this self-assertion to puberty, these finding-out-for-yourself maneuvers can be disastrous because of your size, mobility, sexuality, and strength.

In the teenage group, doing your own thing (acting out) with no regard for the consequences is the common denominator of behavior. Rebellious teenagers are **behaving as** infants *between two and two and a half* who don't yet feel the need for responsibility. When they feel secure, these teenagers can **act like** they are part of the adult society, but when under pressure, or the influence of alcohol or drugs, all pretense of civility and maturity falls away and they act out, sometimes in violence and with the morality of a threatened two-year-old infant—but now they are almost adult in size. If, in addition to acting out, your teenage children identify completely with their gangs, they are in the grip of a compound personality arrest—combining the disruptive defense of the fearful *two-year-old* with the blindly obedient defense of the frightened *three-year-old*, who must submit to the will of the group, no matter what, out of fear of rejection, abandonment, and death.

You can expect delinquent teenagers to justify and rationalize their behavior. If you believe any of their excuses, you become part of the problem.

Ask your teenage children what they want to do and most of the time their answer will be "I don't know." You have asked the wrong question. Teenagers aren't interested in *doing*, but in *being*. Teenagers who act out like two-year-olds are trying to establish themselves as separate persons—their drive is to form a new feeling about themselves. Added pressure on them will only induce them to be more insistent in doing their own thing, in their own way. The only true way to handle teenage delinquency is through prevention. As parents or grandparents, we need to allow our two-year-old children or grandchildren to assert themselves by acting out in a protected environment. This is an essential part of their emotional development. "Solving" our crisis of teenage rebellion can only be done one individual at a time.

The crux of the rebellious teenagers' problem is their self-image. Only as this is upgraded will the teenagers behave differently. By persuasion and threats, you can make teenagers act temporarily more mature, but until they *feel* different about themselves, nothing has basically changed. Emotionally, rebellious teenagers are no different at fourteen from what they were at two or three. They are simply working out the need for exploration that they couldn't satisfy at the age of two and—if they submit completely to the will of their gangs—the need to belong and be recognized by their group that they couldn't satisfy at the age of three.

Teenage rebellion should be distinguished from teenage self-assertion—the natural need of adolescents to assert their growing sense of independence in responsible ways. Such rites of passage as the bar or bas mitzvah, confirmation, and even the social debut in modern society, like initiations and vision quests in premodern societies, are all intended to satisfy this need, to acknowledge and recognize adolescents as new or soon-to-be adults and bring them fully into the society of adults. As parents, you can best meet this healthy assertion of independence on the part of your teenage children by giving them greater responsibility for decisions affecting their lives and the lives of your family, and as your children accept this greater responsibility, greater freedom and privileges as well.

## TEENAGE PREGNANCY

Thirty years ago, in my practice at a primary care clinic in a largely middle-class neighborhood, I used to provide sexually active female patients between the ages of thirteen and sixteen with all the information about birth control that was currently available. My efforts were almost totally disregarded. It was not that most of the girls in this group were oversexed or having sex just for the fun of it, they simply *wanted* to get pregnant. Eventually, I identified the drive motivating their behavior. It was the need to gain an identity; the males involved weren't important to them at the time.

Twenty-five years later, as a doctor working for the Arizona Correctional System, I observed the same drive in the sexually active teenage girls of the prison population. The one trait both groups of girls had in common was a very poor self-image.

By becoming pregnant, the girls began to make significant decisions in their lives—often for the first time—and hoped to gain a position in society. By conceiving, the girls declared themselves to be biologically mature; as mothers, they hoped also to establish their identity. Pregnancy meant that a male was or had been interested in them, if for only a brief period of time. They were having something uniquely theirs, their own babies.

In actual practice, the girls' hopes proved to be fantasies. These teenagers had become pregnant when their natural drive to procreate combined with their need to gain an identity—here arrested *around the age of three*. Because their self-image had been formed, in however stunted a fashion, in the first two and a half years of their lives—and fixed in the first six—they couldn't develop past their childish personality arrest. Motherhood would only accentuate their emotional inadequacies.

## EMOTIONAL AGE AND SEXUAL EXPRESSION

Without a strong sex drive, most higher animals would disappear from the earth. All healthy animals (including humans) have a definite need for sexual expression—sometimes urgent, sometimes less so. The sex drive in humans is moderated by age, health, and opportunity, but most of all, by our inner vision of ourselves—our self-image.

I have found that problems with sexual expression are basically problems with interpersonal relationships that go back as far as early infancy. Our feelings toward the opposite (or same) sex are established very early in life, years before we reach puberty, but may not be expressed until much later. Our ability to express ourselves sexually depends upon our ability to form intimate relationships—and this in turn depends upon our self-image—how we *feel* about ourselves.

Those whose emotional development is *blocked* in infancy or early childhood can sexually express themselves only as threatened infants or young children—with total disregard for the rights or feelings of others, as in the case of child molesters and rapists. Rapists, whose emotional development has been severely arrested *before the age of six months*—most often in the first two months of life—represent the most extreme inability to relate to another human being. Rapists depersonalize and degrade their victims so they can exert their frustrated power and rage over them; the greater the rapist's rage, the greater the chance that the rape will end in murder. Child molesters **behave as** *five-year-old* children who can skillfully manipulate others for their own benefit. This in no way excuses the exercise of violent, traumatizing, antisocial behavior, no matter what the motivating feelings. An older child or adult inherently has a sense of right and wrong, and the social information to support it. It means, however, that unless and until the personality arrests are recognized and removed in such emotionally arrested people, we cannot expect them to change.

A thirty-year-old man will most likely seek a thirty-year-old woman for sexual fulfillment. However, if this man's self-image causes him to feel inadequate in his approach to females his own age, he may seek, and feel emotionally equal to, a fifteen-year-old girl. If he feels that the fifteen-year-old girl is emotionally more mature than he, he may approach a little girl, usually within his family, where he feels safe. If physical contact with females is more than he can handle, he may express himself sexually by "flashing."

Again, there is no such thing as abnormal human behavior (or abnormal human sexual behavior) except in brain-damaged or psychotic individuals; there is only human behavior—however unacceptable it may be. Sexual behavior has various levels of expression that are related to the developmental emotional age of an individual, and this behavior may be arrested at any stage.

What is unusual about two-year-old children running through the house displaying themselves? At what age might you expect children to play I'll-show-you-mine-if-you-show-me-yours? At what age do teenagers start making out with other teenagers?

If a gay man under stress has trouble relating to another man his own age, he may be quite comfortable with a younger man. If a younger man is threatening, he may feel safe approaching a teenage boy. If a teenager is too much, he may feel equal to a small boy. We all express ourselves sexually where we feel most comfortable.

In general, we pretend to be more emotionally developed than we feel we are. We can consciously believe in the image we attempt to portray, at least for a time, but when we feel threatened, this charade falls away and we behave at our true emotional (or sexual) level.

As a prison doctor, I attended a unit of child molesters; although it was not my primary job, I worked extensively with some of these men. They emphatically expressed how inadequate they felt with women. Those who were released and later were returned usually stated that they had sex with their wives and girlfriends until they felt under stress, then their urge to be sexually active with children returned and was irresistible.

The only real remedy for child molestation is prevention —promoting the emotional growth of *all* our children from the day they are born. Child molesters suffer from a deeply rooted, compulsive personality arrest. No matter how profoundly they regret their actions, no matter how earnestly they wish, promise, or vow to change, they cannot; threats, beatings, jail time have no effect. Neither does any therapeutic method now available. Until child molesters can be successfully treated, the only responsible course of action is to keep them from *ever* coming in contact with children.

## USE OF PROSTITUTES, CASUAL SEX

For some men and women, when life is going well and they find themselves comfortable with their spouse or partner, their sexual relationship is agreeable, but when problems arise, putting them under stress, their sexual relationship suffers. Fearing that their partner may find them inadequate or may even reject them, they seek new sex partners among prostitutes or casual acquaintances with whom they need make no pretense or meet any standard. They are looking for someone with a lower self-image than their usual partner's, so they can relax their guard and be truly themselves. They use casual sex or sex with prostitutes as a defense against their fear of meaningful interaction, intimacy, and commitment.

I have placed the fear of intimacy at *two to two and a half* on the Smith Index (see page 24). Whether individuals with this type of fear are straight or gay, they will never let themselves be put in a situation of closeness with another. They are protecting themselves against the pain of intimacy once gained but then lost—or never gained at all. The natural state in infancy is to be open, loving, and trusting. Infants are lovable because they accept us as we *are*, without making a judgment. Those who don't allow themselves to get close to another are **behaving as** frightened infants *between two and two and a half* who never bonded with another person or who bonded, only to lose that bond.

If you as a parent have problems with authority, you may have trouble establishing a close relationship with your two-year-old son or daughter. At the age of two, infants are at their peak in establishing themselves as separate individuals. During the times they are asserting themselves in search of their individuality, you need to recognize and reasonably accommodate them in order to prevent their healthy self-assertion from turning into aggressiveness or depression—both defenses against the fear of intimacy.

## SEXUAL ABUSE OF CHILDREN: INCEST

Incest most commonly involves a father or stepfather, a brother or stepbrother, or a trusted male family member who uses a female child as a sexual object for his own erotic stimulation. The real injury and residual hurt is not the physical trauma—the body can heal without significant residual damage—but the feeling of rejection and degradation resulting in the child's lowered self-image is everlasting.

Suppose an uncle, who has the implicit trust of his little niece, seduces and abuses her. The child enjoys and is flattered by being an important person to her uncle, who sets her up and then trashes her self-image by treating her as a mere sexual object. This abuse (rejection by a meaningful person) devastates the child's life, destroying the positive feelings she has about herself.

The age at which these first attacks take place is important but less so than the emotional maturity of the child when she was first assaulted. In general, the less secure a child's self-image is, the greater her need for acceptance—and accordingly, the greater the damage and the hurt when she is betrayed.

In our example, the likelihood is that the young girl's feelings of self-worth will be permanently stunted by her uncle's attacks. Throughout her life, the abused person will **behave as** an unworthy child who merits only an insignificant place in society. She has accepted and will perpetuate the suggestion that she is unimportant and *deserves* to be used. Often such a person, because of her feelings of unworthiness, will later become the "popular" girl (an "easy lay") or a prostitute. If her personality arrest is infantile, she may become a drug addict; if her personality arrest is childish, she may become a kept woman or call girl. Either way, her self-worth is dependent on what she can do for her keeper or customer.

Unfortunately, sexual abuse of children, especially within the family, is much too frequent. Many of these children grow up totally blocking or denying their traumatic experiences. For the most part, they make a fair to good accommodation in everyday adult life. When, however, they find themselves in a new, safe environment—when they form their own family, for example—they may begin to remember some of their former abuse. At this point, the abused person needs an understanding and accommodating partner or professional assistance to help guide and support her, to allow her to understand and overcome the personality arrest that had been suppressed for so long.

## EMOTIONS AND THE TREE OF LIFE

Your roots are intermingled with those of countless generations of your ancestors. Your birthright is the collective knowledge and experience of the human race dating back to its very beginnings—transmitted to you through your chromosomes and genes and expressed by your drive to live and procreate.

The clearest evidence of your birthright is your sense of intuition—simply knowing because you *know*. Through the years, your emotions, which represent your life energy, can either expand or contract—they can grow tall, strong, and full like an oak or they can become stunted and distorted like a bonsai tree in a small pot.

If you are raised in a safe, loving environment, if you receive *acceptance* in the fullest sense of the word, you can reach fulfillment. If, on the other hand, you are thwarted by rejection, this threat to your existence will cause you to stunt your emotional development by forming defenses.

When you are accepted for who you *are*, then joy, excitement, sexual expression, wonderment, experimentation, enthusiasm, compassion—all become automatic. Acceptance allows you to develop love and achieve fulfillment.

When you are rejected, your fear of abandonment and death drives you to form the defenses of hate, jealousy, resentment, racial intolerance, defiance, aggressiveness, rage. Through these defenses, your fear "protects" you from other people (imagined threats). Each of these emotional hang-ups serves to imprison you in an infantile or childish state of reaction.

Your emotions represent your personal power or energy. Each is expressed automatically—registered instantly and represented by a reaction throughout your autonomic nervous system. You can divide your emotions into two primary groups: (1) emotions that move you toward fulfillment; and (2) emotions that arrest your development of a better self-image.

The first group is invigorating; the second group—your defenses, which serve to protect you against a feeling of rejection—wears down your body and prevents further emotional development.

Intuition is the sap of the tree of life; it puts you in touch with all your ancestral past and gives you unlimited creativity, while rejection drains this sap out of the tree. Fear, anger, and defenses impede or stop the flow of creative sap in the tree of life, which, deprived of sufficient nutrients, becomes as dwarfed and distorted as a bonsai tree.

Emotions are energy. When your energy is dissipated by learned defenses, you don't develop emotionally beyond the level of a child. If, however, your life force is not thwarted or blocked during your development, you will have the energy to become a fully mature and evolved individual—warm, open, and loving.

## SUMMARY

Your **self-image**, **emotional defenses,** and system of beliefs are established and all but completely fixed during the first six years of your life. From then on, your emotional responses are predictable; as an adult, anytime you feel threatened or under stress you fall back on the defenses and beliefs you formed when you were an infant or child.

Whether arrested in **infancy**, **childhood**, or both, your self-image acts through your defenses and beliefs to define each of your social interactions—from participating at school, joining a teenage gang, and sexual expression to worshipping, loving, and marriage (or divorce).

Only by letting go of your defenses can you resume your **emotional development**, upgrade your self-image, and lay claim to the energy, creativity, love, and fulfillment that are your birthright.

# 6

# Understanding Your Behavior

## TWO VIEWS OF HUMAN NATURE

In order to understand how you behave, you need first to understand your nature as a human being. There are two opposing views of fundamental human nature, which can be stated as follows: (1) humans are basically warm, open, and loving—therefore you need only to let your inner nature develop to its fullest; (2) humans are basically evil and selfish—the Calvinistic belief—therefore you must dedicate your life to controlling and overcoming your base human instincts.

From my observations and analysis of many, many patients, I have concluded that in our natural state we have a basic desire and capacity to be warm, open, and loving, that we aspire to unguarded intimacy, but that our lives have been filled with threats to our physical and emotional survival. When fearful and threatened, we automatically defend ourselves by withdrawing, hitting, name calling, arguing, domineering, hating, and the like. These learned defenses are provoked by fear in response to specific, perceived threats.

In therapy, some of the most "dysfunctional" people I have encountered are those who attempt the greatest control in their lives. As you work towards complete self-control, you emanate a feeling of control over everyone around you—and you become incapable of allowing others to be near you. The less you trust yourself or others, the more you must control that "evil nature" within them and within yourself. Your attempt to control others will send them the clear message that you don't trust them or accept them as they are.

Compare a super-controlled, opinionated adult to a warm, open, and loving child. Which do you think is more representative of our true human nature?

The antithesis of control is awareness and accommodation. As your awareness increases, your openness affords you more options and you realize that nature and the world around you are ever more supporting.

Ideally, you would have never developed the need for defenses, but rather would have allowed yourself to acknowledge your emotions and awareness. Take the emotion of anger, for instance. The primary purpose of anger is self-protection. If it were used only for truly life-threatening situations and then only for the briefest periods necessary, the cost to your body would be negligible. But when your anger is the least bit sustained, it goes beyond its primary purpose and drains your body's energy. If you can accept your feelings and have a safe environment in which to express them, then you can have your conscious and subconscious energy going in the same direction. This is the essence of living. When you have it "all together," you can accomplish it all.

## WHY—OUR BLESSING AND OUR CURSE

We are blessed and cursed with a conscious, thinking mind that forever tries to explain everything logically. The people who reared you during the first six years of your life—your parents, older siblings, and teachers—all insisted upon explaining everything. They defined the world (mostly falsely) for you, and you accepted their dictates, suppressing your own valid feelings and your own intuitive knowledge, because you needed to be part of your family or group.

Your ability to think and feel—and to act on your thoughts and feelings—is what makes you a human. Scientists are working ceaselessly to unravel the astounding complexity of the brain; they have determined and mapped the regions that specifically control parts of your body, your thinking, your emotions, and your behavior.

In right-handed people, reasoning, short-term memory, and logical, computer-like thinking emanate from the left hemisphere of the brain; emotions, long-term memory, and creativity emanate from the brain stem and the right hemisphere. Home to your subconscious mind, the right hemisphere and brain stem serve as a repository of information about everything that you—or your ancestors—have ever experienced or learned. Your "right brain" works on fuzzy (intuitive) logic mainly by amassing billions of like bits of information to formulate complete, composite images. Your "left brain" uses formal logic and reasoning, much like a digital computer, to analyze and solve problems. Civilization is largely the product of our left brain, with all its curiosity, reasoning, and asking *why*.

To understand the left brain and the conscious mind, you ask *why* things are the way they are. To understand the right brain and the subconscious mind, you ask *what* things really are.

In our public life we encourage and reward those who ask *why*, who use and act upon logic to achieve their goals. But when you apply logic to your personal life and emotions, the results are disastrous, not only for yourself and your family, but for society as a whole.

Asking *why* is both our chief blessing and our chief curse. It implies that there is an immediate, evident logic to the situation at hand. We ask *why* the brakes don't work or *why* the books don't balance. Asking *why* is the way we understand common, everyday problems and the way we arrive at common, everyday solutions. However, when you get away from situations that are scientific, mechanical, or logical and instead consider situations involving people's emotions, asking *why* doesn't increase your understanding. Quite the opposite, searching for logical reasons in feelings, reactions, and defenses will *prevent* you from understanding people altogether. An emotional defense is in fact logical—but only the *first* time it is used (the initial sensitizing event). The second time and every time thereafter, it is a conditioned response—activated without thinking, without regard to the *current* (objective) circumstances. You can uncover the "cause" of the defense only by understanding the original situation, when it was *first* used—not by applying deductive reasoning to the *current* situation (the "effect").

From the time you take your first breath (and even before you are born), you are asking *why*. As soon as you become aware of your environment, automatically you try to explain it. Every time you ask *why*, you must supply an answer. The answer you reach can be no better than your grasp of the total situation *at that moment*. When you ask *why* as a three-year-old child, the information you have—and your understanding of it—are those of a three-year-old. If as that child you form an emotional defense (personality arrest), you will **behave as** a three-year-old *with no greater information or understanding* every time your defense is invoked—whether you are twenty, thirty, or ninety years old—for as long as the defense remains in place.

Picture a thirty-year-old friend, say a former college classmate of yours. He is extremely intelligent, well informed, and attractive, but he is indecisive and cannot make up his mind. And because he cannot make timely decisions, he loses out on job opportunities, on getting a girlfriend, on choosing a career.

If you ask *why* your friend is indecisive, you get nothing but excuses and rationalizations from him—and from yourself. If, however, you examine *what* is really happening, the dynamics become crystal-clear. Look at your friend's behavior—his words, his expression, his actions tell you that, for him, making a definite choice will be final (fatal), that if his decision isn't perfect, he will have to suffer the consequences for the rest of his life. He is **behaving as** a frightened child. If, through age reenactment, you were to look deeper, you would see that as a small child your friend learned it was safer to make no decisions than to make decisions that displeased his parents or older siblings and therefore risked rejection or abandonment.

Your friend's indecisiveness makes no sense in the current situation. The response doesn't fit here. His reaction is not to any real threat in the present—it is a replay of an incident from the *past*.

Using age reenactment with many hundreds of patients, I found a common (almost universal) source of indecisiveness in adults—it is a young child's fear of making any decision, no matter how slight. The fear is that of a threatened child *between two and a half and three*.

Asking *how* and *why* is fine for scientists, engineers, and philosophers, but to understand emotional defenses you need to limit your inquiry to asking *where* and *when* these defenses were understandable and appropriate. You will always find this to be so in the first six years of life, for in those first six years you developed your lifelong image of yourself (your self-image) and your place in interpersonal relationships.

Suppose that, instead of your friend, you are the indecisive adult. As a child between two and a half and three, you needed to explore and be free to try every door, turn over every rock, climb every chair, change your mind—and your decisions—every thirty seconds. Instead, you were thwarted by domineering parents or older siblings, who only approved of decisions that agreed with theirs, who demanded, through repeated frowns, angry criticism, putdowns, and punishment, that you suppress your natural curiosity, your natural need to decide. This is the "cause"—the "effect" is your indecisive behavior in school, in the job interview, and in the bedroom.

To change your indecisive behavior, you need to recognize the fear behind your defense; you need to *reenact* the event that aroused your fear and that first led you to form your defense years before. Maintaining your *adult* vantage point, you need to view this initial sensitizing event, first, as a child of two and a half with your limited personal information and, second, as part of the family group and their interactions.

When you were two and a half, the only facts you had were those you could gather through your senses—sight, smell, hearing, touch, taste, and intuition. Your understanding was the understanding of a two-and-a-half-year-old. What you made of the facts of your senses was the "cause" of your defense (refusing to decide), which, under the circumstances you faced *then*, was understandable and appropriate—for a *two-and-a-half-year-old*. When replayed as an adolescent and later as an adult, this defense became the altogether inappropriate response of indecisiveness—the "effect."

Through age reenactment, you can bring all your years of observation and experience since the time you were two and a half to bear on your emotional defense. Because your subconscious mind remembers everything, when you relive a traumatizing event, you can objectively see your father, your mother, your brothers, your sisters, the time of year, the physical, emotional, and economic state of your family. As an adult, you can understand that your family was preoccupied with economic necessities, physical illness, ongoing competition and hostility—compounded by a host of other problems. You can understand how your family's dysfunction interfered with their ability to support and care for you, and how, as a child between two and a half and three, you had to protect yourself against the threat of rejection and abandonment you perceived every time you made a decision on your own—by refusing to decide, by being indecisive. And you can understand that, far from helping you adjust for your own good, as they suggested at the time, your parents and older siblings were projecting their own maladjustment onto you.

## TRUSTING YOUR INTUITION

Your subconscious mind stores a permanent record of everything you hear, see, smell, feel, taste, experience, or learn. It has inherited all the collective species-saving experiences of your ancestors; it is tuned into a universal mind, the source of all creativity. Just as swallows are born knowing how to build their nests and salmon knowing how to return to their place of birth to spawn, so you as a human being are born knowing everything your ancestors knew. Your senses (smell, sight, touch, hearing, taste, and especially your intuition) are the channels to access the ancestral information encoded in your brain. You become truly alive in the present when you allow your intuition to be fully aware of your surroundings.

Say you are wrestling with a problem that seems to have no simple, straightforward, logical solution. Seek the answer in your intuition, in your subconscious mind. Before going to sleep, review once more everything you know about the problem. Then, trusting your intuition, sleep on it. In the morning, accept the solution your subconscious mind presents you. Don't try to dissect or question it; your conscious mind cannot comprehend the intricacies of a solution integrated by the intuitive powers of your subconscious mind.

Not only can your intuition improve your ability to function in life, but it is also your only reliable means to strengthen your self-esteem, as you upgrade your self-image.

At birth, you do not have a fully completed nervous system and cannot express what you know. But this doesn't mean you aren't fully aware of the universe. The total experience of the human race is encoded in your brain. As nature's most advanced animal organism, you inherently have the most advanced memory reserves to draw upon. Your intuition is the very essence of you, the part of you that can tune into the complete history and experience of all who have lived before you.

## A SAFE PLACE

A safe place is a healing environment that allows you to be yourself; it lets you discover new approaches to understanding your emotions, which in turn allows for growth. The greatest difficulty in creating a safe place for yourself is that you are your own most severe critic. When you feel you are being attacked, the identity of the aggressor matters little—parent, teacher, preacher, child, spouse—the feeling is the same. No one, not even yourself, can command or order a change in your emotional response because it automatically invokes a defense reaction. By attempting to force yourself to change, it may seem that you have overcome an undesirable trait, but under stress you again return to your original reaction—it is still there, controlling you. Any sensation of disapproval or reproach, no matter how small, constitutes a threat and you react by withdrawing.

Nevertheless, you have already experienced a degree of security just by surviving into adulthood and, through trial and error, have learned—or can learn—to reach a safe place, whether by yourself, with a close friend or counselor, or in a support group. When you were an infant or child, the damage you risked by exposing your feelings might have been devastating, but as an adult, you know that, at least in your safe place, you can expose your feelings without serious risk. Each time you do so, you become increasingly reassured.

When, as a parent, you identify and begin to release your personality arrests, you become more accepting of yourself, and your self-image improves. And when your self-image improves, you expand your safe space and can rid yourself of controls, which in turn allows your children to feel safe and to rid themselves of those same controls. It is like repotting root-bound plants, moving each of them to the next larger pot and thus giving all of them room to grow and mature to their fullest size and strength.

It is common to find in therapy that, as grandparents relax and mature, pressures on their children and grandchildren are also relieved, resulting in significant benefits for three generations, even though no direct therapy was given to the other two.

## COMMON SENSE

Common sense is ordinarily considered a good quality. But just what is common sense? You may have known people who have been intellectually bright, yet they seem to lack common sense. Suppose two equally alert individuals, one with common sense and one without, are each going for a solitary hike in the back country.

It is a beautiful, early spring day. The first person, a professor on sabbatical, immediately senses how peaceful the deep forest is and enjoys the exercise of walking along the path in the wilderness. Because he is free of the interruptions and academic commitments of life at the university, he soon becomes engrossed in solving the backlog of problems he has stored in his head—and oblivious to his surroundings.

The second person, a journalist between assignments, sets off in another part of the same forest at the same time. She lets herself tune into every sound and smell that surrounds her. She feels the shifting of the breeze and the dampness of the air as she walks through the low valleys. She is aware of all sensations and sounds; she sees every tree and observes every branching path.

A sudden storm engulfs the mountains at dusk, and sleet comes quickly. Which individual do you think will most likely get out of the woods unaided?

This is what common sense turns out to be—awareness of your surroundings. When you are fully aware of all the information available in any given situation, you seldom make foolish decisions.

## PASSAGE OF TIME

Why is it that when you are small, you can hardly wait for your next birthday, but that, as you get older, life rushes by faster and faster and there isn't enough time to do anything? Your perception that time speeds up is of course an illusion. Children live almost exclusively in the present, while as people age, they tend to emphasize the past and the future to such an extent that they become quite unaware of the present.

Suppose you are out walking your two dogs. The first dog is your old friend of fifteen years; the second is your nine-month-old pup. Your old dog follows at your heels, paying close attention to where you go. The young pup scampers about with untiring enthusiasm, chasing a rabbit down the path and a squirrel up a tree, running around every bush, and sniffing at each tuft of grass. Which dog do you think has the fuller experience?

This is what has happened to you. You no longer smell the rich, damp earth or hear the crackle of twigs underfoot. You are almost entirely inside your head. On the walk, your emotional energy is spent on solving problems, on rehearsing your role in upcoming events, and very likely on reliving past hurts others have caused you. The only part of the present you are aware of is the weather (and perhaps the ache in your lower back).

In other words, you reside almost exclusively in your *conscious* mind, which blocks your subconscious. You are making judgments rather than observations, and because you are living in the past and future, the present—and therefore time itself—eludes you.

## ALCOHOL, DRUGS, AND SELF-ABUSE

Like all living organisms, your body is equipped with biological systems of checks and balances. Each system, almost without exception, has the ability to increase or strengthen, as well as to decrease or lessen, the functions or sensations it governs. Drugs and medicines can greatly stimulate or suppress the abilities of these systems, although they cannot get the systems to do anything they could not do unaided.

Alcohol, angel dust, aspirin, cocaine, heroin, nicotine, novocaine, morphine—all suppress one or more parts of your brain or nervous system while stimulating, or not directly affecting, others. Angel dust (phencyclidine or PCP) can loosen fantastic thoughts, not because it directly stimulates the brain but because it depresses some parts while selectively allowing others to overact. Aspirin, by suppressing your body's inflammatory reaction to tissue injury, lets the rest of your body feel better.

Alcohol is the all-time favorite suppressant because it obscures moral values, memory, and social learning, so that our coarser, more primitive drives can come to the fore. By suppressing the higher, moralistic part of your brain (which distinguishes you as human), as well as your awareness of your physical surroundings, alcohol lets the primitive part of your brain (which you inherit from your prehuman progenitors) become overactive, which you may often interpret as "having a great time." By drinking, you give yourself permission to do chemically what you wouldn't let yourself do intellectually.

Alcohol is sometimes thought to stimulate sexual abilities; it may seem to with some people because inhibitions and morals are blunted and raw sexual desire predominates. But after drinking any significant amount of alcohol, your ability to perform sexually, just as your ability to talk, walk, or drive, is impaired. And after as few as two drinks, the quality of sex changes; intimacy becomes increasingly blocked as subtle feelings and communication disappear. The more you drink, the less sensitive you become to other people.

The primary purpose of pain is to protect you against further injury. Novocaine (procaine) and morphine suppress your sensation of pain so that you can use your body in spite of injury. Being rejected is the worst pain or hurt we can feel. Heroin is one drug especially designed to block this feeling; it gets its addictive power from its ability to free the user from this most severe pain—rejection. When the drug's effect wears off, however, the pain of rejection returns, causing addicts to crave another fix to again free themselves from their torment.

I find the current term *substance abuse* altogether inapt. Cocaine and alcohol certainly don't care what their "abusers" do with them. I suggest we think of "abusing" nicotine, heroin, alcohol, or any drug in personal terms—as *self-abuse*. It is the *abuser* who has a problem—not the substance "abused." By calling addiction what it is—"self-abuse"—we keep the focus where it belongs, on the addict, and may increase the chances that addicts will receive the help and counseling they need.

There is overwhelming evidence that any number of substances, some of them perfectly legal, can with prolonged use induce physical dependency (causing nausea, tremors, craving, and even epileptic seizures when they are withdrawn).

I suggest that *all* addicts (self-abusers) are greatly dissatisfied with their basic self-image. Addictive substances all have the ability to alter, obscure, or obliterate their users' self-image. With paint sniffing and designer drugs, their use seems unconsciously calculated to permanently destroy the hated self-image.

Detoxification in a safe place is indispensable. Later, however, unless the addict can upgrade his or her self-image, the effect of treatment is totally lost. Each time the addict returns to drugs reinforces the addict's feelings of "unworthiness" or "worthlessness." Current failure makes long-term failure a self-fulfilling prophecy.

To recover, addicts must feel the desire and make a conscious decision to change their lives, but they will succeed only in an environment where they feel safe to grow (such as Alcoholics Anonymous). To try to force them physically or emotionally to change their behavior is totally futile.

## SECURITY AND THE GENERIC PERSON

Can you picture any place in this world that is free from all possible physical disasters, such as fires, tornadoes, floods, hurricanes, lightning, earthquakes? Is there anything you have that can't be taken away from you?

Nevertheless, one of our favorite illusions is security. Security in the commonly accepted sense is actually a defense, and like all defenses, it will trap you and limit your life choices. Everything you do repeatedly becomes automatically controlled by the housekeeping functions of your subconscious mind. When you repeat a task over and over, your conscious mind is no longer exercising new choices; you are running on automatic pilot. The more you follow a routine in your daily life, the more you limit—or eliminate—your true choices.

As a society, in our pursuit of "security," we seem to have drifted into a state of minimizing creative choices. More and more, we are relinquishing our power to take risks, choose, decide, and run our lives in favor of "safe" routines and vicarious experiences. More and more, we are careful to do what we have always done, while—in books, on TV, in the movies—we read about or watch *others* face challenges, risk, and danger and make serious choices to survive and achieve their goals. Day after day, we consciously suppress the imaginative, creative portion of our subconscious minds to maintain a "safe" status quo for our self-images. Like generic products on supermarket shelves, we are becoming generic people, neither good nor bad, but somewhere in between—indistinguishable from one another.

At two, you are at your maximum ability to switch ideas, actions, and directions; you never stay with any one thing long enough to accomplish much. As you grow older, you narrow your focus and increase your persistence so that you can actually complete the projects you begin. If, however, when you are *three years old*, your parents and older siblings repeatedly urge you to adopt excessive constraining limits, to override your creative and decision-making abilities, you learn through fear to go along with them, to suppress your imagination and intuition. And if, as you pursue "security" in later years, you further restrict your creativity by adopting conforming routines, eventually you become a generic person.

All you can be sure of in this world is that things will change, no matter what you do—or choose not to do. The only true security you can have is confidence in your ability to adapt successfully to change. Your ability to deal with change is directly proportional to your open-mindedness—your awareness—and your trust in your intuition to make sense of the information gained through awareness.

The stronger and more mature your self-image—the freer from personality arrests of any kind—the greater your self-confidence. And the greater your self-confidence, the greater your true security.

## SELF-DESTRUCTIVENESS, SUICIDE, AND THE ENDING OF LIFE

Self-destructiveness is the expression of a two-year-old personality arrest. When infants *between two and two and a half* feel they don't belong in their family or group, they are driven to do what they aren't "supposed" to do. We have all known or heard of these "accident-prone" children. They are always exposing themselves to unnecessary risks, which most often evokes an immediate reaction from their parents—they get attention.

This trait only appears when infants feel inadequate to compete. As the children grow older, their abilities and resources for risk taking also increase. The adolescent who drives at excessive speed and the adult who drinks and drives have the same two-year-old personality arrest of self-destructiveness. They don't care about themselves, they aren't "worthy" of consideration, and therefore nobody else is worthy of their consideration either.

Their conscious minds can protect them from their subconscious drive for self-destruction only until they feel their stress is overwhelming. Then, they commit suicide—or, as is more often the case, they expose themselves to one unnecessary risk too many.

The ending of life can be a carefully thought-out decision, almost free of emotional imperatives. When you reach this conclusion, it is with calculated consideration for those around you. When you feel that your quality of life, because of illness or deterioration of your abilities, is diminishing, when you realize the hardship and pain that you, your family, and your friends must endure because of it, you may elect to end your life as a carefully considered, conscious decision.

## INTUITION AND THE ACCEPTANCE OF REALITY

Self-esteem is what makes you an individual. Your self-esteem is based on *believing and acting upon your intuition*. Each time you choose to act solely on logic, each time you override what you intuitively *know*, your self-esteem goes down.

The principal purpose of this book is to help you overcome the fears, anger, and defenses—your self-imposed controls—that keep you from being your true self, and trust more and more in your deep intuition. This is possible only if you let go of your fixed ideas of how the world should be and how people should act.

You cannot develop emotionally if you insist on defending or justifying what is already in your head. Most of your present conclusions are valid only for the conditions that prevailed in the past. You cannot adapt to the changing world if you cannot change your ideas.

You often hear people say, "I can't buy that," "That can't be," or "I can't believe that." When you have a set idea or picture in your mind of how the world should be, you are not seeing the world as it really is. You cannot change the world, but you *can* change your *perception* of how the world is.

The world is not necessarily good or bad, it just is. To be realistic in the best sense is to be in tune with the world as it exists, to accept the "unacceptable" when it occurs. If your father has died, he is gone. If your mate has committed adultery, that is the way it is. No amount of crying or anguish will change it. A period of shock, pain, or anger is expected and understandable, but the longer you deny reality, the longer you delay getting on with the rest of your life. Accept what has happened and adjust to it. Accepting reality is the first step in healing.

## ULTIMATE FREEDOM: *BEING*

Considering the age, extent, and forces of the universe, we occupy a very brief and limited place. Our bodies can survive only in the narrowest range of temperatures, compared to the extreme coldness of outer space and the extreme heat of the stars, including our sun. Our physical strength is insignificant, compared to the forces that bind the atom together and that blow the stars apart. The physical forces around us are the major external limiting factors of our lives.

As an infant, you learn early on to accommodate to gravity when you walk, climb stairs, or sit on the edge of your chair. You learn to keep your hands away from hot stoves and to pull up a blanket when you are cold. These physical forces neither reject nor accept you, they just are. All forces outside of us keep us in a degree of physical bondage, for we must accommodate to them before we can learn to live within their confines.

Immigrants come to the United States seeking more freedom than they had in their native lands. Beyond economic advantage, they seek the freedom for themselves and their children to *be* all they can be, to use and develop their individual talents to the fullest.

The degree of *voluntary* bondage you have chosen for yourself is plain from your actions. When you act as if you "should," "ought," or "must" behave in a certain fashion, you circumscribe your life, you limit your freedom to *be* yourself. No one else in this world can curtail your freedom to be a unique person as severely as you do by the self-image you have adopted. People around you can prevent or limit you from *doing*, but you are the only one who can adopt and support the image of who you can *be*.

You gain the five essential freedoms—to *think*, *feel*, *choose*, *imagine*, and *live*—only when you allow yourself to *be*. The freedom to *do* is secondary and is always limited by environment, time, place, energy, and the permission, to a greater or lesser degree, of those around you. To be truly free means that, even though you remember and are guided by the past, you aren't *limited* by it.

When you grow *beyond* your personality arrests—when you allow yourself to *be*—you are free to live your life joyfully, abundantly, confidently. You greet life and the world around you with a sense of humor and appreciation. You are free to recognize and acknowledge differences between people —and to respect those differences, without the need to control, manipulate, interfere, or judge. As your awareness grows, so does your natural sense of responsibility toward others; you are free to give and receive help, to support your own growth and the growth of others without competitiveness or condescension. You are free to express your own feelings and sexuality and to allow others to express theirs. Open to genuine intimacy, you are free to love—and be loved—unconditionally.

Ultimate freedom comes from within—when you relax your expectations, open your mind and senses to the present, and let yourself *be*.

## SUMMARY

Established and for the most part fixed by the time you are six, your **self-image** governs your behavior, reactions, and attitudes. Learning to see these as they really are—without explaining, excusing, or judging them—will help you understand your self-image and the central role it plays in your life.

How you feel about yourself determines your attitude toward—and thus your perception of—the world around you, the common sense you use every day, the passage of time, your freedom, and your security. Your fears and **anger** can make you susceptible to alcoholism, drug addiction, and self-destruction.

As you learn to trust your **intuition**, you will upgrade your self-image and, by gaining the five essential freedoms—to think, feel, choose, imagine, and live—become an open, emotionally mature adult.

Chapters 7 and 8 set forth methods, techniques, and exercises to help you achieve—through relaxation, **acceptance**, **love**, and emotional growth—a fuller life for yourself and your family.

# 7

# Parenting Yourself as You Parent Your Children

## TRAPPED IN YOUR PAST

You may well be uncomfortable with some of the concepts in this book. None of us wants to be trapped in the past. Most of us would like to apply traditional American problem solving to our emotional problems and come up with clear, logical answers. But as you become aware of how you in fact behave and feel, it becomes increasingly clear that just because you are intelligent and can think logically doesn't mean you always do what is best for you.

If rational thinking could solve emotional problems, this world would have been a better place to live a long time ago. Intelligent people wouldn't commit suicide, family members wouldn't murder other family members, and no one would be promoting the arms race.

"You are what you think you are" is firmly entrenched in American pop psychology. In reality, you are what you *feel* (what your *subconscious* mind tells you)—not what you *think* (what your conscious mind tells you).

An infantile or childish reaction is just that, no matter how old you are in years. Acting out unrestrained emotional feelings is perfectly acceptable behavior in an infant or small child, but not in an adult, who should have learned maturity and self-restraint. Of course, no adult likes being called a child, but it is important to remember that our emotional defenses respond to imagined threats from the *past* and have nothing to do with logic or the objective reality of the present.

This applies to cases of severe loss or trauma in adults. Of those devastated by the murder of a loved one, by rape, or by war, for example, some will recover after a period of grieving and some will not, no matter how hard they try, no matter how much time passes. If you suffer from post-traumatic stress disorder, you are indeed trapped in your past by what you experienced—not as an adult, however, but in the first six years of your life. No matter how much your adult loss or trauma exceeds in objective terms what happened to you as an infant or young child, the threats you perceived in the two experiences and your emotional reactions to those threats are similar. The emotional defense you formed to protect yourself back then—rage, bitterness and resentment, depression, withdrawal from the world, whatever it may be—has been activated by your more recent trauma, and will continue to be by your memories of this trauma. Until you release your defense, until you overcome your personality arrest, your ability to cope with adversity of any kind will be severely impaired.

## EMOTIONAL GROWTH

If you try to force change, you will only strengthen your personality arrests. Hang-ups are defenses—if I attack you directly, you will respond; even the slightest attack will provoke your defenses and thus reinforce your hang-ups.

It would be wonderful if all we had to say was "Well, I know now that in the past my poor self-image has been the root of all my problems, so I will just think better of myself" to avoid unwanted behavior and feelings. But changing how you *think* about yourself simply doesn't address the problem—it is how you *feel* about yourself that is fundamental. And how you *feel* about yourself is a hundred or a thousand times more important than how you *think* about yourself. To accomplish any improvement in your life and in how you relate to others, you must alter your subconscious mind, which is not only the repository of your fears, emotions, and defenses but also the seat of your intuition, your assertiveness, and your self-esteem.

Because your hang-ups have been reinforced so many times over the years, you first need to *reduce the severity* of your emotional reactions when you become defensive. Your emotional energy is limited. The major part of your emotional energy is already committed to your "protection" through learned emotional defenses such as violent temper, bigotry, and dogmatism. Only a small part of your energy is available for discretionary use.

When you use almost all your emotional energy to support your defenses and to sustain your social or economic position, you severely limit your options, which consequently prevents you from developing emotionally and from being the parent you want—and need—to be. On the other hand, blocking your emotional reactions altogether will simply redirect the withheld energy inward, where it will eventually destroy your body. Only by changing the way you *feel*, by reexperiencing and releasing your old fears, can you diffuse your destructive energy and free up your positive energy. Only by changing the way you feel can you let yourself—and indirectly your children—grow emotionally.

## CHANGING THE PICTURES IN YOUR SUBCONSCIOUS MIND

The goal is not to eliminate the unwanted pictures stored in your subconscious mind—which in any case would be impossible because the subconscious forgets nothing—but to *change* them. Adding to the information you have already stored lets you look at a particular picture from a larger, truer perspective—to draw a more informed conclusion and to change your past (and therefore also present) perceptions.

Most of us are like the old World War II Japanese soldier who chose to hide away for thirty years on an island in Indonesia rather than surrender. We are still fighting the wars of our early childhood decades after they have ended.

You learned how to survive your childhood battles, as any good soldier must. But you are an adult now, and the time has come to look at your old wounds, understand them, and—by freeing up your personality arrests—allow yourself to heal. You need to reach into your subconscious mind and let the old soldier in you see that your reason for fighting those battles has long since vanished.

## REACHING INTO YOUR SUBCONSCIOUS MIND

In order to communicate with your subconscious mind, you need to quiet your conscious mind—your critical thought. This is the only way to gain entry into the vast knowledge and experience stored in your subconscious.

Your reaction to the event that initiated your emotional defense (initial sensitizing event) was entirely logical and appropriate, considering the circumstances and your perception of what was happening at the time. Your situation now is far different from that first encounter; nevertheless, your subconscious reaction overrides what your conscious mind understands as the logic of the moment. Every time you react defensively, your subconscious has taken you back to when you *first* learned this response. The evidence is all around you. When you observe a family member, a friend, or yourself behaving in a childish or infantile manner, you realize that you are witnessing a spontaneous age reenactment.

You automatically experience spontaneous age reenactment many times each day. By contrast, during directed age reenactment, you *consciously* choose to suspend the reason and logic of your analytical mind, while *retaining* your adult awareness, in order to reexperience—and *reexamine*—the circumstances in your infancy or early childhood that first led you to form your emotional defense (the initial sensitizing event).

Directed age reenactment does not—in and of itself—effect a cure, much less an instant cure. It only opens the door by letting you reexamine how you formed your emotional defense, what made—and makes—you feel and act the way you do, which in turn enables you to understand and accept yourself. You must accept yourself *as you are now* before you can consider growth in your emotions. As long as you resist reliving the original experience, you will remain dominated by it. "You cannot heal what you cannot feel." Your original experience will remain real and active for as long as, unconsciously, you still feel threatened by it. Successful therapy requires that you apply your current awareness to your former situation, neutralizing your old fears by reexperiencing them as they first arose, by adding information with understanding, by forming new pictures (new images), and by *releasing* the feelings attached to the old—thus changing how you *feel* and, in turn, how you act. This doesn't happen all at once. The old images are upgraded slowly; you have spent a lifetime reinforcing them.

A trained therapist can guide you all the way back to the first experience underlying your unwanted feeling or behavior, while creating for you a safe emotional environment, thus allowing you to examine even the most hurtful situations in safety. But there is much you can do on your own. You can initiate self-analysis by becoming increasingly aware of your defensive reactions and what is really happening when you behave defensively. Relate your behavior to the Smith Index (see pages 24–25) to find at what age you first created your defense. By doing this, you can start to lessen the impact of your emotional defenses on your development and you can start to let reason (maturity) into your life.

One good way to begin is to become ever more analytical as you give up being critical. Learn to observe other people's behavior without judging—not as "good," "bad," or something in between, but simply as it *is*. The closer you observe the behavior of others, the more aligned your feelings will become with theirs, and the more you will learn about yourself. As you learn to identify and age-date the behavior of those you deal with, as you learn to deal with them at their actual emotional age level, you will become much more effective in interpersonal relations. This constant, careful observation will reward you over time by expanding your awareness not only of other people but of yourself as well.

Discussing your observations and analyses with a partner or a small group of friends familiar with age-dating and the Smith Index can also be very helpful and supportive. But to reexperience—consciously and safely—the emotions you first felt when you formed your defenses, to release both these emotions and the defenses themselves, you will need the guidance of a therapist trained in the technique of directed age reenactment.There is absolutely no way you can change (grow emotionally) unless you *accept* yourself as you *are* now. Any attempt to explain or justify your reaction in today's environment indicates that you aren't yet feeling safe enough to allow yourself to grow.

In the past your parents molded your character based on their own childhood experiences. You cannot now remold yourself (change your self-image) into what you would like to be, until you remove all impediments—all personality arrests—that prevent you from maturing emotionally.

## HONESTY

The first and perhaps the hardest step in reducing the impact of your emotional defenses is acknowledging and dealing with yourself *honestly*.

For forty-five years I considered myself a truthful, honest person. As far as keeping my word or being honest at the checkout stand or not cheating on my taxes, that was true. Honesty (in this commonly understood sense) was a family tradition, and I thought myself to be the staunchest member to uphold it. I also condemned those who used a lesser standard.

As long as I considered only rules, regulations, and protocols, I could maintain my pious stance of honest conformity. But when I finally gained insight into my feelings, I found I had been anything but honest. From earliest childhood I had been taught that boys didn't cry, get frightened, or ever show they were afraid, that anger was sinful, that you didn't talk about love or affection or show you cared by hugging family or friends.

Adapting to my family meant not only suppressing my feelings, but denying their very existence. For forty-five years I acted as if living up to my family's standard was more important than expressing what I really felt. I discovered that, as an emotionally shut off person, however much I "upheld" my reputation as a forthright member of the community, I was being totally dishonest with myself.

There are two simple ways you can identify and acknowledge your true feelings. First, make note of what you see as faults in others, for what bothers you in them is really what bothers you in yourself. Your intolerance of a particular trait in another is there because in your infancy or early childhood someone—most often your parents—condemned this trait in you.

Second, if you have children of your own or have been closely associated with growing children, you may have found that at certain specific ages their behavior became intolerably annoying to you. Make note of this, too. You can be quite sure these were the same ages *you* were unacceptable to your parents, when *they* couldn't tolerate your behavior and consequently disapproved of you. You took on their disapproval and adopted it as a true standard, and you certainly are not going to allow any child to have the same obnoxious traits. Know that, by feeling and acting as you do, you are only perpetuating your *own* personality arrests, passing them on to another generation.

When your children act out, recognize that *they* believe they are experiencing a crisis. Remove them, if you can, from the present situation to a place where they can feel safe enough to give up their reaction and thus reduce the chances they will form a permanent emotional defense. Consider how you might feel toward a two-year-old little boy, a total stranger, who is lost in a department store. Would you scold him for crying and screaming, for not staying with his mother, or would you comfort him and make him feel safe? Almost certainly, you would reassure him that his mother would be there soon and that everything would be all right. Find the child within you, who may also be frightened and lost. Comfort and reassure your child. Make your child feel safe.

## EXPECTATIONS

There is only one cause of all the anger and stress in this world—*unrealistic expectations*. Expecting what is inappropriate and excessive will cause you to be upset, as eventually all your fantasies result in bitter disappointment. On the other hand, if you expect only what is almost sure to happen, you will have no conflict, aggravation, or need for defensive action.

If you expect your twelve-month-old son to be toilet-trained and he wets his diapers, there is nothing wrong with your son, *you* have the problem—you expect him to be more emotionally mature than he is.

If you expect your mother to treat you as an equal rather than talking to you the way she did when you were a child (even though she has talked to you that way all your life), *you* have the problem. You expect her to be more mature than she is. She will never treat you as an adult because she has always seen you as a child. In her mind, you simply haven't matured, and she's not about to relinquish her "control" over you. (This is her five-year-old personality arrest.)

You love your father and want to give him the perfect gift. You decide on matched luggage for his upcoming trip.

You heard him talk about color, size, and all, so you know exactly what kind of luggage he has in mind. When you present the gift, he criticizes everything about it, and you get upset. There is nothing wrong with your thoughtfulness or with the gift. The problem is your *expectations*. If you had used all the information available to you since you were a child, you would know that he criticizes everything and everybody—nobody pleases him, not even himself.

In all of these instances—and in all your relationships—the only thing you can really change are your expectations. Because you had unrealistic expectations about your son, your mother, or your father, you became angry. Your anger didn't change your son or your mother or your father; what it did was to make them feel uncomfortable to be near you. You felt rejected by who they were, not for who *you* are. In reality, your anger may sometimes get you what you want, but it never gets you what you *need*; it always turns back on you, affecting, most of all, your own sympathetic nervous system (in a destructive way).

See others as they are and expect only what is going to happen anyway. When you are relaxed and feel safe, you allow yourself to grow emotionally—and you allow others, especially your children, to feel safe and to grow emotionally as well.

## BASIC STEPS FOR CHANGE

1. Identify the unwanted behavior or feeling.
2. Recognize that to improve, you need to allow for change.
3. Accept that human nature, if allowed to unfold, is basically good.
4. Understand that any conscious effort to force change will create an even stronger resistance to change.

5. Replace control of your conscious mind with direction of your subconscious.
6. Give yourself space.
7. Know that you have the answers.

## GUIDE FOR PARENTING

All your daily activities are guided by feedback: when driving a car, you make constant corrections in your steering to stay on the road; when singing, you have a reflex that allows you to correct your pitch to stay in tune. You also have feedback for parenting, but much of your children's emotional development will not be apparent for one to six years, too late for you to alter it; what you learn from them later can only be applied to your grandchildren.

In parenting, you rely on the information and feelings you have at the moment. If you also gather the collective experiences of others or, better still, truly understand your own emotions, you can apply your acquired learning and knowledge to retrain yourself, to allow each of your children to have an independent and positive self-image.

Your chief job as parent is to provide a safe place for your children to develop emotionally. Recognize first that you can't change what is inherent in your children. Like every living creature, their potential is already determined at birth. But even though you can't alter or increase their potential, you can easily distort, stunt, or arrest their emotional development. Your highest calling as parent is to protect and allow your children to flourish—by encouraging and supporting them as they develop their talents and capacities to the fullest.

As you come to realize that your own fears, anger, and defenses stem from your experiences during the first six years of life, as your awareness increases and you learn to better accept yourself, you can better support the emotional development of your children, giving each of them greater opportunity to develop a desirable self-image and emotional maturity.

## Accept and Love Your Children

For the most part, discipline is a pitiful substitute for affection. Every person wants to be accepted and loved. If, from the start, you accept and love your children as they *are*, they will be free to choose to act naturally. Your children's needs are best met and their chances to develop emotionally are greatest when you make them always aware they please you just by being themselves.

Your newborn children can't express themselves verbally, but you can easily learn to understand *without* words when they are hungry, what they like or don't like to eat, when they want to be held, and when they need to have their diapers changed. Let them choose from all the (safe) choices available, but avoid extending their choices endlessly just to please them or gain their approval. When your newborn daughter, say, stops feeding after only a few ounces of milk, respect her decision. Project the same feeling of love and acceptance you do when she empties the bottle. In this way you are teaching her to trust herself, to respond to her body's natural signals, and to grow in self-esteem.

Be aware that your infant children want to be a part of the family. During the times of the day your family is together, bring your babies over and hold or prop them up so they can easily see and hear what is going on. You will discover how eager they are to participate; soon they will begin to make sounds and movements to express their interest and excitement.

Each morning, let your schoolage children choose which clothes to wear to school (from those you and the school find acceptable) or which breakfast cereal (from those you have available) and how much cereal they wish eat. Or suppose your young children are outside jumping in the puddles from a summer storm. You know the mess their clothes are going to be, but you also understand the fun they are having. Allow them a few more minutes before you call them in. After they change their clothes and are warm and dry, find some time to sit with them and share their excitement and pleasure. And when your children—or someone else's—resist being hugged, kissed, or held by an adult, honor their feelings. They may not wish to express their affection in that way, or they may not even like the adult being pressed upon them. Make them feel okay by accepting their feelings, whatever they may be.

You can readily express your love for your children without words; the more you explore nonverbal communication, the more your children will feel your acceptance of them.

## Set Reasonable, Impartial Limits

Every second of your life you must come to terms with limits imposed upon you. Even before you were born, in your mother's womb and passing through the birth canal, you experienced limits. When you let yourself learn about limits, life becomes a constant succession of choices, and you are able to handle whatever situation you encounter. This same natural process needs to prevail in rearing children. When reasonably and impartially imposed during the first six formative years, limits can be be as natural for your children as the physical reflexes that slow them down when they are out of breath.

The real secret is to impose those limits as impartially as, say, a brick wall around your backyard. When your young child runs his or her tricycle into the wall, the pain will soon go away and the scraped elbow will heal with no lasting effect—except that your child will have learned respect for the wall. Limits help children mature and become part of society. These limits should be reasonable, impartially imposed and constantly adjusted for your children's age and sense of responsibility. Most of all, the limits should be announced *beforehand*. No child will dare develop emotionally if called to account for breaking rules announced only after the fact.

Your children need no discipline, but they do need to know what is expected of them and what their limits are. Healthy children will continue to test their limits and naturally try to "beat the system." This is good as long as they respect the rights of others and assume responsibility for their actions.

As a parent you set limits to your children's behavior, which expand as the children grow up; without these, children can't feel safe. You provide a safe place by gradually expanding your children's limits to allow them to use all of their ever-developing capacities. Limits give them a sense of familiar territory, a safe place to grow, so they don't have to concern themselves with an unlimited number of things that might cause stress as they learn to understand and deal with their human surroundings and associations.

When someone accidentally hits your face while you are playing a game, you soon forget about it. But when someone you love slaps your face in anger or derision, the sting of this rejection will stay with you for years, perhaps forever. The chief lesson parents teach children in anger is *fear*. Discipline in the usual sense amounts to retribution.

The true art of parenting is to impose limits without anger or malice. What harms your children—and can devastate them—is not imposing limits, but doing so *in anger*, which children take as *rejection* from someone they formerly trusted. The firm word or the whack on the buttocks you give them when they misbehave needs to be as impartial as getting burned by a hot stove or banging into a wall. If it is, the lesson is learned and the limit accepted—with no harm done. But if it is delivered in *anger* (rejection), this will cause a lifelong scar.

An angry or inconsistent parent can only teach fear. After acceptance, setting limits impartially and reasonably (without anger or malice) is a parent's second most important job.

## Have Faith in Your Children

Your children have as their birthright the knowledge and instincts that assured the survival of our ancestors through countless generations. What they need to grow and develop, to become emotionally mature adults, is to trust themselves. They can gain this trust only if you have faith in them, only if you allow them to make their *own* choices. If, instead, you usurp their decision making, you are teaching them to feel inadequate; you are teaching them to be afraid.

It is a long-standing observation in the medical profession that twenty percent of the people consume eighty percent of medical care. Much of this demand for attention is rooted in infancy and early childhood. If you have always been tuned into your children intuitively, there is no qualitative change in the attention you give them when they become ill; it is simply more of the same mutual understanding. However, if your children sense they get much closer, more caring attention from you when they are ill than at any other time, they learn a technique to receive special care and attention they will use the rest of their lives.

Faith in your newborn son or daughter to grow into a strong, emotionally mature adult is like faith in an acorn to grow into a sturdy, full-sized oak. You can't make your children into what you want for yourself—or into anything they aren't—but you can, by having faith in them, allow them to fulfill their potential.

## Stick to the Affirmative

Before the age of three, children's ability to use critical judgment or appraisal (conscious mind) is minimal. In the first three years their behavior is governed almost entirely by instinct and emotional reactions (subconscious mind). An infant can learn to walk and to understand the word "walk" and its opposite, "wait"—but not the *negative* concept of "don't walk."

Children become confused, uncertain, and fearful when the commands of their parents or older siblings are delivered in anger, frustration, hostility, or fear. When children are told, for example, "Don't touch," they subconsciously recognize the action "touch" but, far more strongly, they feel the emotions projected subconsciously by the one giving the order as disapproval.

You seldom listen to and register every word you hear. You form an idea of what is being said not only by the words you hear but by the emotions you perceive behind the words. The emotions you transmit when speaking reflect your true feelings. When addressing your children, whether to praise them or to reprimand them, they will understand your projected feelings more strongly than the words you use. There is no need for you to shout, demean, or use profanity when reprimanding your children; they will instinctively know you disapprove by the feelings you project.

One of the best habits to establish as a parent is thinking of and expressing your commands in the affirmative. For instance, if your two-year-old son is headed in a dangerous direction, you might call, "Wait there," which is an affirmative command; then you might take his hand and say, "Come along, let's go in this direction." The child will interpret an affirmative command simply as information—devoid of the feeling that he is being attacked. Later, when your son is a little older, you might also explain very simply why one direction is preferable to the other.

If, however, your command is in a negative form (for instance, "Don't cross the street!"), you will induce a defensive reaction in your son even before he understands your words; the more you confuse and frighten your child, the more timid and unassertive he will be.

Infants can gain confidence in themselves only when their world—and especially their family—is working with them. When parents project their disapproval, anger, or resentment most of the time, their children will be doubtful, unsure, and confused most of the time.

Consider how much simpler, clearer, and more effective the affirmative forms of the following examples are than their negative counterparts:

| | |
|---|---|
| *"Don't walk in the puddles—you'll get all wet."* | *"Stay on dry ground and your shoes will stay dry."* |
| *"Don't lie to me!"* | *"Tell me the truth!* |
| *"Don't be so mean to your brother!"* | *"Be good to your brother!* |
| *"Don't play in the street or you'll get run over."* | *"Play on the grass and the sidewalk only—away from traffic."* |

To change your mind-set and habit pattern as a prospective parent, you can begin with the practice of stating everything in the affirmative, even before the birth of your first child. You will find this to be a remarkable exercise, for you will realize how often you use negative expressions of all kinds. As you continue to practice the affirmative form of expression, you will notice that your communication improves not only with your children but also with adults.

## Talk to Your Children Eye to Eye

In communicating, the first and perhaps the most important thing is to be a good listener. Your baby can't talk, your young child can't always find the right words, your teenager won't always seek you out, so you must use all your six senses to tune into what they are saying *without* words. In order to be a good listener, and an intuitive feeler, you will need to get back your emotional energy; to do this, you may have to give up some of your fixed beliefs and defenses—just as you might have to return your new car or your credit cards to pay for something really important.

When communicating with children, you will be more successful if you do it eye to eye—at the same physical and emotional level. Recognize their emotional age and the extent of their understanding, whatever their age in years. To attempt any new word or act, your children need to feel okay about themselves—and about you—and safe with their surroundings. Make sure they are comfortable and get comfortable yourself (which, if your children are very small, may mean sitting on a pillow or lying down on the floor).

As you talk with your children eye to eye, make physical contact with them in whatever way feels natural to you and them. Your feelings will be transmitted far more powerfully by your touch than by your words. Tune into your children's feelings, state them, and allow your children to express them. With infants who can't yet speak, just let your warm and caring emotions flow toward them with soft words and reassuring tones.

As your children acquire verbal skills, encourage and reinforce these by introducing new words and ideas to them. Speak with them at their level of understanding, but avoid using baby talk and silly words, which your children will (rightly) feel are condescending. A good way to support them and instill confidence is to repeat (mirror) their words and phrases back to them. Always end your dialogues by showing how glad you are to have shared this experience with them, how much you like them, and how you accept and love them as they are. Young children don't always spontaneously demonstrate their affection with hugs and kisses; just be open, warm, and receptive as you demonstrate yours.

Two people speaking different languages may have trouble communicating, but they can succeed if both use patience and great willingness to understand. So it is between parents and children. If you expect your two-year-old daughter to behave according to adult standards, her actions will be as hard to understand as if she came from an exotic land. Likewise, if you try to communicate on an adult level with your 130-pound, five-foot-five teenage son who has a two-year-old personality arrest, you are not likely to get very far. If, on the other hand, you talk to your daughter and your son as they *are*, as two-year-olds making their first stand at developing an independent individuality (at their emotional level based on their *actual* behavior), then you will have no more difficulty communicating with them than with any two-year-old.

## Teach Your Children by Example

No two people have equal abilities in all areas; we each have a few things we do or know especially well. This also holds true when you are communicating with your infant children. They aren't equal to you in life experience or analytic intelligence, just as you aren't equal to them in unrestrained curiosity, desire to imitate or learn, or willingness to trust. There is very little you need to actively teach; when your children are emotionally ready and free of stress, they will eagerly imitate almost anything they see you do and adopt as their own almost anything they sense you feel. This is clear in children's phenomenal ability to learn whatever language their parents speak, including accent, dialect, speech mannerisms, and intonation, no matter how complicated or subtle.

If you are like most of us, you hope your children will learn how to behave better (more thoughtfully, more maturely, more wisely) than you—from somewhere else. In reality, they will learn how to relate to others, how to express their feelings, their sexuality, their caring almost entirely from you, not by what you say or think, but by what you *are* and *feel*—by your *example*. Depending on how you feel toward them, your children will feel good or bad about themselves and consequently form a strong or weak self-image.

So you have a choice. You can teach your children fear or anger by being fearful or angry yourself, or you can teach them understanding by your example—by *being* patient, respectful, and responsible. Children learn fear and anger as readily as they do language or table manners, forming emotional defenses to "protect" themselves from encountering or being harmed by a fearful object, person, or action ever again. But they learn patience, respect, and responsibility just as readily, if more gradually.

To teach your children fear or anger is to handicap them as surely as if you had maimed their bodies. They will never use those emotional parts and talents they have locked in the "safety" of their fearful or angry defenses.

By contrast, to teach your children by your example to be understanding, respectful, and responsible is to leave them free to live their lives to the fullest.

## Encourage and Support Your Children

Most of what you do throughout the day is a reaction to the information stored in your subconscious mind and a direct projection of your self-image. You act first and think later. If it were not so, getting through a single hour would be an intolerable burden because your conscious mind lacks the capacity to plot your every action. In general you act instinctively, using your subconscious mind, and your conscious mind only justifies what you have already done.

You make the best decisions you can considering the information you have at the time. The hardest decisions are those which require you to override your impulses with your reasoning. Many times even before you finish a sentence you wish you had given it more thought. How much more do some of us wish we could have reared our children differently if only we had the information and experience then that we have now.

Start by setting aside the concept of right and wrong. Replace it with the idea of free choice and "cause" and "effect." Each of your choices ("cause") leads to certain results ("effect").

Some choices have terrible repercussions.

Other choices lead to productive lives.

The bottom line is that you do only what you *want* to do. You need to be aware of the consequences of your choices and to accept responsibility for the choices you make. See your children's behavior as it *is* rather than as *you want* it to be; understand what your children do without approving or disapproving, excusing or condoning.

If you choose to spank your two-year-old daughter, it will have a very definite "effect" on her future behavior. If, instead, you choose to encourage and support your daughter, you will have directed her in another channel. Neither choice—in and of itself—is right or wrong; they just produce different "effects."

Like almost all of us, you love your children and want them to have a better and more fulfilled life than you. Thanks to modern technology, they will probably have physical advantages you didn't have, but you, almost alone, will be responsible for your children's emotional growth; you, almost alone, will determine whether your children are encumbered by personality arrests or believe in themselves and feel free to live their own lives. Your responsibility as parent is to see the potentials in your children and to nurture and foster these to the best of your ability.

Your children come into this world with capacities and limits but with no self-restrictions and self-distrust. Provide a safe place for them to grow emotionally and protect the good feeling and confidence they have about themselves.

Start on day one. Treat them as emotional equals. They are born with knowledge. Recognize this. Give them a head start by letting them make their own choices. There are thousands of little ways you can support them.

Listen to your children and watch them intently. When they start to do something, avoid doing it *for* them (remember, you don't have to prove yourself). Instead, give your children the least amount of help they need and encourage them to succeed on their own.

When your children stumble or fall down and hurt themselves, encourage them to start again as soon as they can, before they lose interest. Acknowledge their bruises or bumps and their feelings about them, take care of their minor injuries if you need to, but add as little energy as you can to their self-pity. Express your love and acceptance of your children as they are, whether they succeed or not, but avoid excessive or inappropriate praise, which only serves to undermine your children's self-esteem and which can become addictive.

See the potential in your children. Teach your children to believe in themselves. Know that how you feel toward them will be how they feel toward themselves. They are precious, but they are yours only in the sense that you can spend the most time and have the most experience with them. They are not part of you. They are *themselves*.

Encourage your children to try and try again. They will only learn by mistakes and false starts. Support your children when they try, and especially when they fail, for only by trying, making mistakes, and trying again can they acquire self-confidence.

## SUMMARY

During the first six years of your life—provided your parents support your natural instincts and don't inflict their fears and **anger** on you—your emotional growth is automatic. After the age of six, further emotional growth is difficult, but still possible.

Before you have children or when you have very young children is the time you need to understand yourself and to pass the emotional benefits on to your children. As a parent, you cannot push your children to develop, however much you try. But you can, by dealing with yourself *honestly*, by recognizing and releasing the defenses that are blocking your own emotional growth, lead the way for your children to proceed with theirs. You teach your children by example, by what you have learned and practiced. When you speak to your children only in affirmative terms, when you encourage and support them, you confirm your **acceptance** of them. Believing in your children as equal individuals helps them believe in themselves.

# 8

# Techniques and Exercises

## CONTROL

In order to leave yourself open for emotional growth you need first to relinquish any attempt to control. Control is a myth—you can control your conscious mind, but never your subconscious mind (which manages ninety percent of your bodily functions and controls *all* your emotional reactions). You were told to "control" your emotions, your life, and other people. In reality, you can control none of these, especially not your emotions (except to suppress their outward expression).

## UNDOING SHOULD, OUGHT, AND MUST

If you hear the words "should," "ought," "must," "try," or any variation in your thoughts or in what you say, this is a clear indication that you are stuck, though perhaps only partially, on a *three-year-old* emotional level. These words represent the conditioning you received in your early childhood. Your parents introduced them into your command center to make you dependent so they could direct you in what they thought you should do or how your should live. In this three-year-old subservient role, your sense of self is completely dependent on what others think of you.

To say that you "must" do something implies that if you don't, "they" will disapprove or reject you or will try to deprive you of something. The truth is that you don't "have" to do anything—you can refuse to do anything if you are willing to pay the consequences for your actions.

Whenever you use the words "should," "ought," "must," "try," or any variation in asking something of another person, you may intend to command that person, but in effect you are putting him or her in charge of you. Whether it be your friend, your boss, or your lover, the other person remains in charge for as long as your "need" exists. In a good friendship or marriage, on the other hand, both partners feel equal and free to ask—not "command"—each other to do any number of things, directly, openly, and without manipulation; asking and complying carry no threat of obligation or domination but are instead mutual sharing.

Take a piece of paper and write these phrases one right under the other: "should do," "ought to do," "try to do," "must do," and any variation that comes to mind. Reflect on them. All of these expressions amount to commands, whether to others or to yourself, yet all of them make you subservient, dependent on the other you "command" in the present or the parent who "commanded" you in the past. They are all lies, and every time you use these words, you are lying to yourself. Every time you obey these commands, your self-esteem (and therefore also your self-image) goes down.

Instead of using "I should do," "I ought to do," "I must do," and the like, say "I *choose* to do." At first, making this simple substitution might sound trivial, but in truth when you substitute "I choose" for "I should," "I ought," or "I must," you are automatically changing your status from victim to volunteer. Likewise, when addressing others, instead of using "you should do," "you must do," and the like—instead of "commanding" others—*ask* them directly, forthrightly, "Will you do . . . for me?" "Will you go . . . for me?" and so forth. Stand behind your request and give the ones you ask the opportunity to *choose* to comply. These simple changes will keep you and others from being defensive and will help free up the emotional energy you and they have invested in defenses.

Be aware that if you have a running grudge or contempt for another person, you are putting energy into this emotion and it has control over you. You choose to be a perennial victim, for each time that other person makes a move, you must make a countermove. You are no longer a free agent.

When you are a victim, someone else is always running your life. But when you are a volunteer, you are in charge; if you do something for another person, you do so willingly, as a matter of choice. Depending on your attitude, the way you feel and the stress on your body are amazingly different. As we have seen, tiredness is most often not fatigue or exhaustion but merely a sign of stress. You are forcing yourself to do something you don't *want* to do—you are doing it grudgingly, with conscious effort. You are, for example, tired of taking out the garbage for someone else because you feel coerced. But when you *choose* to take out the garbage, you do so not as a frightened, resentful three-year-old dependent on what others think of you, and not as a grumbling, rebellious five-year-old, but as an *adult* who chooses to be part of the family. When you volunteer to do the chore, the physical energy expended is the same, but the emotional energy required for resistance and resentment is saved.

## RELAXATION: FLOW VERSUS CONTROL

Relaxation is your natural state. Tension drains your energy and, more often than not, diminishes your ability to deal with danger, challenges, and life itself. To be a champion golfer or any other accomplished athlete, you need to react only to the situation immediately at hand and allow your subconscious mind, which is itself guided by your accumulated past experiences, to direct your body's learned and practiced functions. To be at your best, you need to flow—to be fully alert, ready to move in grace, and relaxed in all that you do.

To appreciate the inhibiting effect of conscious control—with its resultant tension and stress—choose a familiar indoor staircase with at least a dozen stairs, preferably one that is carpeted and has a handrail, and stand at the top of it facing down. Normally you walk down this staircase without thinking and with minimal effort. But now try walking down the stairs *controlling* each step. Shift your weight to the left foot, bend your left knee as you lift your right foot slightly and move it forward the width of the tread. Lower your right foot the height of the step and smoothly shift your weight to it. Consciously repeat these maneuvers until you have gone down twelve steps. I can almost predict that you will stumble before you reach the bottom and that, in any event, you will be under considerably more stress than you were at the top of the stairs.

Almost everybody agrees that there is a basic need for relaxation, but few of us actually allow ourselves to relax—least of all, those who are most in need of relaxation. Every once in a while your mind and body need to relax, to escape the constant mind battles and dialogues going on in your head and to recover from the physical and emotional strains of your life. If you feel you need to relax, do it. Relaxation is automatic as soon as you disengage your expectations of how the activities of that minute should be and allow the world to be as it is. When you give up the need to consciously direct every action, you will move quite naturally, smoothly, and correctly on your own. As you trust yourself more, you will become less anxious—and more relaxed.

What is important is that you clear your conscious mind so that you can become more aware of yourself and your surroundings. *Let* yourself relax; forcing yourself serves only to provoke self-argument and defenses. Your conscious mind, with its logic and reasoning, is not the cause of your problems. If you could by logic change yourself, then altering your emotions would be no more difficult than getting a tune-up for your car. Your adjustment problems are in the *emotional* part of your makeup, which is governed by your *sub*conscious mind. To change your subconscious mind, you need to circumvent or at least temporarily suspend your conscious thinking.

To achieve real change in your life, you need first to satisfy your sense of reason that what you are about to undertake is for your growth and under your direction, that it will lead to your personal fulfillment and to more meaningful relationships with others.

Basically, you need to recognize that, just as with all living organisms, when allowed to be *yourself*, unfettered and unimpaired, you will develop to your best natural state. If you accept the premise that your emotional development was arrested by the defenses you formed in your infancy and early childhood—and that, by letting go of those defenses, you can resume your development—then you will find the following exercises helpful.

## CENTERING

Select a relatively quiet area, sit up straight in a chair with your feet flat on the floor, and allow your hands to rest on your thighs, palms up. Close your eyes and tune into your breathing. Pay attention only to the exhalation phase of your breathing and allow your chest to relax so that you are letting, not forcing, all the air out with each breath. Your breathing will slow because your exhalation is prolonged.

Just as relaxing and breathing easily are the opposite of feeling defensive, so deep inhalation breathing and breath holding are the opposite of relaxation. Your first reaction when suddenly threatened is to take and hold a deep breath—you automatically do this the instant you perceive danger. You need to have a maximum amount of air to scream, run, attack, or steel yourself for an oncoming attack.

Next, listen to the silence around you. There will be many sounds that intrude. Resist any temptation to react to these noises—or to analyze or explain them. Just let them be.

Allowing things to be is one of the most important acts of your life. As your awareness grows, you realize you don't need to change, modify, correct, or react to everything you perceive. Eventually you will want to limit your reactions to only what is essential or desirable for you. Remember, the only thing you can truly change in the world is your perception of it.

If you find that thoughts tend to crowd in and compel you to respond by analyzing them, you can block your conscious mind by jamming. Repeat some meaningless word or sound over and over, something like "Aahum" or "Tabatabadum," first out loud, then softer and softer, and finally just in your mind. Repeat it for fifteen or twenty minutes as you continue exhaling completely with each breath. You don't need to put any effort into inhaling, for that comes automatically.

## RELAXING, RECONDITIONING, AND HEALING

Using the indented suggestions below, make a tape in your own voice and your own words and listen to it each time you want to perform this exercise.

When threatened, whether you are going to attack or be attacked, to run or scream, you always start your defenses by taking a deep breath and holding it. In contrast, here as in the centering exercise above, you will practice letting all the air *out* of your lungs, which is essential to obtain maximum relaxation. With this technique, your defenses recede, and with them your level of stress.

Again, choose a relatively quiet place and sit in a comfortable position with your eyes closed, with your feet flat on the floor, and with your arms and hands resting comfortably on your thighs.

- Let the air out, out, out, and relax. Know that when your body needs oxygen, you will automatically inhale. Relax, let the air out, out, out. Let your lungs deflate and allow your chest to become as small and as flat as it can naturally be. When you breathe out,

out, and out, you notice that your throat also relaxes. Your nose and sinuses open and you are able to breathe more easily. Let your head sag and your shoulders droop. You notice your hands become heavy on your thighs as relaxation engulfs you. Let out all the stress as you breathe out all the air from your lungs.

- Just as the bubbles of carbon dioxide, when you open a bottle of club soda, rush up from the bottom of the bottle all the way to the neck, so tiny bubbles of carbon dioxide, when you breathe out, rush up from every cell of your body, from the most distant parts of your body, from your toes, from the tips of your fingers, through your bloodstream all the way to your lungs, where you breathe them out. Let the air out, out, out.

- At the same time, let your shoulders droop and your head sag as you feel more and more relaxed. You are in a safe place, a safe place for letting yourself relax and go unguarded, even if for only a little while. As you let your guard down, you notice the silence that surrounds you. Tune into this silence. As you become more aware of the birds singing, your own breathing, a car in the distance, or a telephone ringing, recognize all these sounds and simply let them be. You are learning the secret of paying attention only to what is important—yourself. Let all these unimportant sounds go by. As you relax, your hearing becomes sharper and your awareness more acute. Let all these things outside you be. Pay attention only to the silence and the relaxation in your body. Relax deeper, deeper, deeper.

- You become very comfortable as all the tension goes out of the muscles in your back, just as it did from your shoulders when you let them relax. The only important thing right now is to relax, deeper and deeper. As your hearing grows sharper and sharper so do your other senses, and you become more and more aware of the other parts of your body.
- When you feel a tingling in your arms and legs, think of the tiny bubbles of carbon dioxide rushing up from the cells in the distant parts of your body through your bloodstream. All this carbon dioxide is going toward your lungs, where you breathe it out.
- Each time you relax your chest, you can go deeper and deeper and deeper. As the air goes out, out, out, your chest and lungs go all the way down.

With this relaxation technique you can tune into each part of your body separately. Focus particularly on those areas of your body that are ailing or hurting in some way.

- Tune into your right big toe, your left ear, your waist, your lower back, feel and identify that special part of your body that is troublesome in some way. Feel the carbon dioxide escape from the cells of this part, feel the pain and discomfort flow out into your bloodstream and rush toward your lungs, where you breathe it out. Your exhaling breath takes it out, out, out.
- As you tune into the troubled part of your body, your distress flows out and is carried away by the tiny bubbles. Where you feel tightness or swelling, tune into that part of your body. Feel the bubbles of carbon dioxide escaping, the tightness and swelling flowing away, and feel healing take their place. As

you relax more and more and more each time, you breathe out more and more stress from this troubled part of your body, and natural healing takes its place. Your body is healing itself on its own. Whether you feel tension in your back muscles, swelling or soreness in a joint or somewhere else, let that area relax. As you relax, you increase your circulation, you let the toxins clear away, and you allow healing to take place. This happens as you relax deeper and deeper and deeper. You increase the healing as you relax more and more. You convert the energy required for tightness and swelling into healing energy.

You may use this technique to tune into any part of your body. If your problem is emotional, think of it as being like a tangle in a fishing line. Your thinking has been tied and knotted by stress and the emotion that keeps you unsettled. When you relax and let go, your subconscious mind has the ability to heal, to untangle the snarl in the fishing line.

- Just relax, let your consciousness drift out of the way, and let natural healing proceed. Relax and let your subconscious mind unravel and loosen your worry knots. You are aware that stress created your knots; now your subconscious mind is undoing them as you relax. Let the air out, out, out, go deeper and deeper every time, and relax every part of your body.
- Have a moment of silence here, and all the while let yourself relax and let your lungs go as flat as they can go, completely relax. When you need to breathe, you will do it automatically.

*(Be silent for ninety seconds.)*

You tend to consciously override many of the natural responses in your body. By clearing away your confusion, you automatically pay increasing attention to the sensations within your body. And as you tune into your body, you will reawaken its natural responses and realign its natural regulatory functions.

You will, for example, be able to recognize once again the natural sensation of hunger, the physiological imperative for eating, which will become your *only* clear signal to eat. You will eat slowly so that, once again, you can recognize the natural sensation of **satiety**, your body's sense of having eaten enough, which will become your clear signal to *stop* eating. As you return to your natural state, you will eat only when you are hungry. When your hunger is satisfied, you will stop eating and let no one talk you into eating more.

The more you align yourself with your body's natural responses, the stronger these signals will grow. Each time you relax, you automatically increase your awareness. Just as your hearing becomes more acute than usual when relaxing, so will your other senses become sharper and the feelings in your body become accentuated.

- Now tune into each part of your body, one by one, from the tips of your toes to the top of your head and everywhere in between. Relax and let everything go until you become realigned with your body's responses. Let yourself go deeper and deeper and deeper.

*(Be silent for thirty seconds or as long you need.)*

Conclude each relaxation, reconditioning, and healing session along these lines:

- Allow yourself to come back up feeling refreshed and energized. Bring your head up, open your eyes —remember everything in this session that is useful to you.

Do this exercise on a daily basis. Make a recording in your own voice, using some of the ideas in the passages above. Incorporate whatever you feel will fulfill your needs into your personal tape.

State everything in the affirmative and the present tense. You are working with your subconscious mind, which recognizes no negatives and only one time—the present. In formulating affirmations for yourself, avoid any that require *doing* anything, such as "you have to," "you've got to," or "you must"; you have had such demands foisted upon you all your life. Instead, make affirmations that allow your natural growth to resume, that foster natural understanding, development, and healing—that focus on your *being* everything you meant to be. You might begin with an affirmation like this: "You know simply because you know. Your intuition has been passed down to you through thousands of generations. You trust yourself."

## AGE-DATING PERSONALITY ARRESTS

To age-date behavior you observe in yourself or in others, first select the most salient action in the behavior and place it in one of these two categories:

**Infant**: Birth to two and a half years old

**Child**: Two and a half to six years old.

The observed behavior belongs in the infant category if it is focused on the *self*, whether for self-preservation or self-gratification; it belongs in the child category if the behavior is focused on *others*, whether to dominate or submit to them. Next, consult the Smith Index (see pages 24–25) for the behavior pattern closest to what you observe and note the particular age associated with that pattern.

Say your boss comes back to work after lunch and brusquely orders, "Somebody get me a cup of coffee!"

Moments later, slamming his fist down on his desk, he barks out, "Where the hell is my coffee?"

Does your boss's behavior belong to the infant or the child category? He wants satisfaction—personally and immediately. He is therefore **behaving as** an infant. Immediately —an infant cannot wait. Profanity (meaningless talk to express anger or displeasure)—*two to two and a half years old*.

Your boss's behavior is infantile—self-centered, with no concern for others. To put his personality arrest in sharper focus, review what history you can learn about him, recall all his past behaviors and all the stories he has told about his past experiences that exemplify his attitude toward others.

You can't "solve" your boss's problem, nor should you try. If you confront him, he will only act *more* like a two-year-old; active interference may even get you fired. Instead, acknowledge to yourself that your boss's two-year-old personality arrest is entirely *his* problem. If you can't escape the situation, accommodate his infantile behavior as you would any other two-year-old's, but only as far as you need to. In our example, you might bring him his coffee and go about your business. When he calms down, he may be able to **act like** an adult—until he is again stressed.

A mother goes to visit her married daughter, who has children of her own. As soon as the mother arrives, she begins to criticize how her daughter keeps house, tends to the children, and so on.

In which of the two categories do you place the mother's behavior? Obviously, in the child category. The mother believes that her daughter should submit to her—do things the way Mother does them—and any alternative is unacceptable. In this scenario, the mother is trying to reestablish control and reassume the dictatorial role she exercised over her daughter in the past. She is the classic dictator who is emotionally arrested at a *five-year-old level*. If the daughter understands her mother's behavior, she won't feel hurt by it and will be able to deal with it as she does with any five-year-old child.

## MONITORING YOUR DEFENSES

Through the thousands of directed age reenactments I have conducted, I have found a common age of origin for each general category of defensive behaviors and traits. Each of your personality arrests was formed at—and can be traced to—a specific age.

First, familiarize yourself thoroughly with the Smith Index (see pages 24–25). Then, identify the childish or infantile behavior the emotional defense you wish to change. Determine whether it is infantile or childish behavior. Next, fit the observed emotional defense into the proper time in your life when such behavior was appropriate. Check with family or friends who knew you in your youth; they may be able to tell you (or corroborate) the exact circumstances that threatened your life at this time—the age of origin—and that consequently induced your defense.

When you have age-dated one hang-up, look for others at or near the same age. It is likely your home environment had a family disruption about then, so that you were challenged in a number of emotional categories at the same time.

These insights don't automatically change you, but they help expand your awareness, which lets you judge yourself less harshly, or rationalize your behavior less often, so that you aren't constantly berating or excusing yourself. Justifying your behavior or attacking yourself only perpetuates and reinforces your unwanted reactions. You *can* change your behavior, but only when you feel different about yourself, and then only slowly. Such change becomes much more feasible when you understand how you came to behave the way you do.

Each time you are aware you are acting out, take note of your behavior and age-date it. At first, you will drop right into a particular emotional defense before you realize it, but the more aware you become of your defense, the sooner you will be able to recognize it—in the nick of time. Eventually, you may get to a point where you are aware the instant the emotional response starts, and only then will you be able to stop and prevent yourself from acting it out. Later, you may elect to channel the energy in some other direction.

## AGE REGRESSION TO PAST LIVES

Suppose a hundred people are age-regressed and five of this group see themselves in a past life as Cleopatra on a barge, floating down the Nile. Does that prove that all five of them were once Cleopatra? Or does it, more logically, indicate that these five people were all tuning into the common consciousness, all reviewing the same inherited memory, like students reading the same chapter in a common history book?

When I have conducted patients back to past lives, I have often found a situation like the following. A male patient with recurrent ulcer pains sees himself living through an early battle of the American Revolutionary War as a soldier at Bunker Hill. He feels himself receiving a musket ball in his stomach—and may remark, "That's why I'm having so much belly pain now, isn't it?" Well, hardly. More likely, it means that his subconscious mind, searching through his inherited memories, has come upon a particularly vivid one of a person who once shared the same ailment, pain, or feeling.

In all the directed age reenactment sessions I have conducted, I have found a significant incident in the first six years of the patient's present life that is the direct cause of the patient's current defensive behavior. Regression to past lives, no matter whose they may be, provides information devoid of the emotional content essential to effect a change in self-image and emotional development. I therefore consider this type of regression, which can be induced by any competent hypnotist or hypnoanalyst, to be a fanciful pastime; in my experience and as far as I can determine, it has little or no therapeutic value.

## SCREEN DOOR

People can criticize you, call you names, or put you down, but the only way this can affect you is if you put energy into their words. Suppose someone calls you a name in a foreign language. In order for it to affect you, you first have to translate the name, identify something from the past, and put energy into it. Each time you energize someone's verbal abuse, you experience a bodily reaction. The resultant stress, if allowed to accumulate, will age you prematurely and may even contribute to your early death.

Instead, practice *saving* the energy you normally expend in reacting to criticism, name calling, and putdowns. Let this abuse pass right through you like a breeze through a screen door. You will be pleasantly surprised at how powerful the image of the screen door can be—and how much better you will feel when you make use of it.

## A CUP OF COFFEE

All of your anger is eventually redirected toward yourself, where it accumulates as harmful stress. So the next time you become angry, let yourself be aware of your true feelings. Sit down by yourself and have a cup of coffee, tea, or whatever (nonalcoholic) drink you like. Slow down your breathing and breathe all the way out; this will relax your chest and allow much of your tension and anger to dissipate. Imagine that your stress is escaping with each breath out, like waves receding at the seashore.

Identify as precisely as you can what happened (or didn't happen) that made you feel angry. Resist any temptation to feel sorry for yourself and pay no attention to thoughts like "If only . . ." "Why couldn't . . . ?" "I (He, She, They) should have . . ."

Review what did or didn't take place, then identify what you expected—wanted or wished for. Ask yourself, "Were my expectations realistic, or just wishful thinking (fantasy)?"

Go through your memory bank for similar situations involving the same people. What was your and their attitude and performance during the last ten minutes? The last ten years? Is your and their behavior now different from what it has been in the past? Use all the information you have within you.

Reconstitute the just-played scenario with all the information you now have uncovered. What will your expectations be in the future?

After many such moments of coffee and reflection, you will begin to expect only what is bound to happen. From that point on, the moments of anger in your life will begin to diminish because you will be able to apply your growing awareness of reality to your expectations.

The outstanding cause of stress is anger or fear, both of which you create by unrealistic expectations. With anger, you repeatedly or constantly expend your energy on the past; with fear, you squander your energy on the future. From over forty years of observing patients, I have found stress to be one of the major noninherited factors in aging. If even when you sleep, your body is not at rest, it has little or less time to repair and regenerate your tissues. As a result, your aging process accelerates, often dramatically. By reducing your anger or fear, you will reduce your stress and allow your aging process to return to its natural, slow pace.

## BACK FROM THE FUTURE

If you stop to consider, most of the problems you had to face two or five years ago have been resolved one way or another. At the time, you may not have had an active part in their solution, but with the added information and experience of the intervening years, you can easily solve these and similar problems now.

When you were small, say five years old, you noticed that most of the people around you were larger, stronger, smarter, and more capable than you. You may have thought,

"When I get to be as big as Daddy or Mommy (or my older brothers or sisters), then I can do what they do." Getting dressed for school, finding your way in kindergarten, and defending yourself from the class bully may well have been monumental problems for you as a five-year-old. But if you could return to kindergarten as you are today, with your added knowledge, size, strength, and determination, is there any doubt you could solve all these and any other kindergarten problems with ease?

To help solve some of your present-day problems, suspend all logic for a moment or two and imagine yourself projected into the future. You are six, seven, even eight feet tall, superintelligent, experienced, and sophisticated. In your imaginary state, come back from the future to survey a particular problem. Now that you are taller, stronger, and more capable than you were, the problem you once thought unsolvable becomes very simple—as simple as any kindergarten problem might be to an adult.

Imagine yourself at whatever size and level of sophistication you need to be to cope with your current problems. If your first image is inadequate, then reshape the image until you feel that you are large enough, smart enough, and experienced enough to turn your hardest problems into minor difficulties.

With all your acquired attributes, project yourself ahead from the present—one, two, five years—to the time when you have resolved a particular problem or situation to your satisfaction. Focus on the end result; let your imagination draw the picture and fill in the details as to how this is going to be accomplished. Have faith in your intuition. Focusing on the end result—and coming back from the future—will open up a whole world of possibilities. You may well wind up with a far better resolution than what you had pictured initially, and, at the very least, you will discover new and more powerful ways to solve your problems.

## CLONING YOURSELF

Suppose you genuinely wish to upgrade your self-image. There really is no way you can affirm that you are superior, great, the best there is, without your critical conscious mind shouting it down almost immediately.

To circumvent this sabotage of your project, imagine a clone of yourself. Picture a perfect copy of you in every way, shape, and form—with all your feelings, with every fear and every attribute. Now imagine this clone an arm's length away as a small child, helpless, lonely, and unwanted. Let yourself experience this child's feelings. Protect and give this child all the love, protection, and acceptance that weren't there for you as a child.

See your clone as a member of the human race, with all its potentials and opportunities. Accord your clone the same recognition and respect you would the most revered person you know, be it the Pope, the President, or anyone you choose. Think how many helpful things you have done for other people, especially your own children. Now look at this image of yourself as a child. How many helpful things have you done for this person? As you wish this duplicate of your younger self well and every success, automatically your subconscious mind is upgrading the attitude you have about yourself (your self-image).

This technique is especially helpful in dealing with alcoholism and other addictions. If you have a problem in this area, imagine a clone of a little girl, your own or someone else's you care about. Could you pour liquor down her throat or inject dope into her arm? Could you bring her to a back alley, a dive, a crack house, to mingle with drunkards, pushers, and addicts? Yet this is what you have done to yourself, because you have felt you are unworthy. Now imagine a clone of yourself as a young child, and give this child all the acceptance, protection, and love you would the little girl.

Practice time and time again creating this clone of yourself so that it becomes second nature, and you can produce this image in an instant. Know that each time you do this, your subconscious is upgrading your self-image. When you are asked to do something you know will cause harm, imagine, if only for a brief moment, that it is your clone who is being asked rather than yourself. By protecting your clone, subconsciously you are also protecting yourself.

## INFLUENCING YOUR YOUNG CHILDREN

During their first two years of life, infants are adapting to their environment. If their parents are argumentative, quarrelsome, and reject each other or, even worse, reject themselves, these messages will become part of the infants' feelings about themselves and will shape their self-image.

If for any reason your infant children have been exposed to such messages, you may wish to use the following technique to help them heal emotionally. Parents adopting infants should be aware that their adopted children were very likely unwanted or at least regarded with some degree of rejection and are therefore in special need of acceptance and love. Whatever negative messages these children received from their original parents are imprinted onto their self-image and cannot be changed by logical explanation, no matter how patient or well-intentioned. Unless and until their self-image can be upgraded, they will feel unworthy of being loved.

One powerful way to upgrade the feelings your infant or young children have about themselves (their self-image) is to communicate directly with their subconscious mind. You can reach your children's subconscious during the twilight period of light sleep (the first twenty to thirty minutes of sleep), when their sense of hearing is working but their conscious mind is at rest. During this period your children are especially receptive to your projected thoughts and feelings.

Each night, just after your children fall asleep, tell them how important they are, how much you love them, and how special they are to you, to your spouse, and to themselves. But far more important than your words are the feelings you project when you say these words. Your sincerity and affection will be especially transmitted by your touch. As you speak to your sleeping children, stroke their hair or hands with a steady, slow, rhythmic, and gentle movement. Know that you are providing two elements vital to their emotional development: a safe place and acceptance.

Do this three to five times a week to reinforce your children's feelings of acceptance. Remember that your feelings rather than your words will be imprinted, so avoid using this technique on any night you are upset, angry, or preoccupied. Talking to your sleeping children in a truthful, convincing way will lead you to examine your capacity to communicate intimately with others. Your own subconscious will automatically change so that your relationship with your children during their waking hours will be vastly improved.

This technique can be also successfully used with your children of four and above. At bedtime read to them, something you and they enjoy—it doesn't matter what. When they fall asleep, switch to stroking and talking to them in a reassuring and comforting manner.

## YOUR DREAMS AND YOUR DEFENSES

What good are your dreams? What purpose do they serve?

The primary purpose of dreams is to rehearse your defenses—to keep you alive by keeping you away from dangers you confronted in the past and may confront in the future. Dreams maintain your status quo by reminding you of who you are. They are there to help support and perpetuate your self-image (and thus also your belief system). Whatever you feel about yourself (your self-image) is reinforced nightly in these pictures from your subconscious. Your self-image may differ radically from what you consciously *think* you are (your self-portrait), which is nearly always make-believe.

Dreams take place in the short REM (rapid eye movement) periods of sleep about five times each night and occupy about twenty percent of your total hours of sleep.

While you are sleeping, your conscious mind is inactive, and your subconscious mind may then take over.

Primitive societies have rich traditions of legends and customs that are passed down, word by word, from generation to generation. Through this continuous process their members know where and how they came to be and who they are. If these oral traditions, practices, and rituals are interrupted for any length of time, the identity, culture, and customs of these societies disintegrate and may be lost forever.

Your subconscious mind functions much like a primitive society. It renews and reinforces what defenses it has learned, practicing and rehearsing them every night in dreams. But, like subjects in sleep laboratories, if you are repeatedly deprived of the opportunity to dream, you may suffer an emotional and intellectual breakdown.

When you imagine a dangerous scene or have a vivid, threatening dream, your defenses are immediately and automatically activated as if the incident were taking place at that very moment. Your subconscious mind knows only a single time—the present; for it, there is no past and no future—everything is happening to you right now. Your subconscious mind ensures your survival by rehearsing again and again in your dreams those specific defense techniques you first learned in your waking life.

When you undergo therapy, you become aware of new information and gain greater insight, which allows you to mature emotionally. Your subconscious mind will most likely be alarmed and will try to get you back to your old status quo. When you begin to mature emotionally by letting go of some of your emotional defenses, you may evoke dreams that once again make you feel incompetent, inferior, or inadequate.

In such "loser" dreams, your subconscious mind makes up a story in which you feel inadequate or fearful. The cast in your dream may be drawn from people you have actually encountered or from those in the archives of your memory. The time, place, setting, and participants are entirely irrelevant; your feelings and defenses are the only important issues. The basic theme and action are the same, they all reenact and reinforce defenses that protect you from change.

You also have "winner" dreams. The positive sides of your self-image can also be reinforced by your dreams. If you are confident and assertive, you will have dreams to bolster and reassure you. When you allow yourself to change by natural growth instead of attempting to force change by challenging your defenses, your dreams will also gradually shift from "losers" to "winners."

Waking up on the wrong side of the bed is almost always caused by the dream you just experienced. Your dream defenses may be reasserted, for example, to estrange you from someone in an immediate relationship, when your subconscious mind senses you are allowing that person to become emotionally too close to you, provoking your old fears of being hurt, rejected, or pushed away.

Tiredness is probably the most widespread symptom encountered in primary care medicine. It is almost never related to overexertion, whether physical or mental, but is instead the result of stress from consciously forcing yourself to do something you subconsciously don't want to do.

Waking up tired in the morning is a prime expression of conflict. Your dreams evoke defenses, and the stress of conflict is what makes you tired. It is an indication that you need to pay attention to (and heed) your emotions and intuition.

## "BAD DREAMS": REPROGRAMMING YOUR SUBCONSCIOUS

When you have a dream that evokes a fearful or undesired defense reaction, sit up in bed, recall the dream in detail —write it down if you can. Then, analyze what is going on in this dream, but attach no meaning to the identity of the players, colors, background details, and so on. Instead, identify the action in the dream and your unwelcome emotional response.

Deal with the problem right then and there—before you go back to sleep—consciously rejecting anything that caused you to feel in any way at a disadvantage. Use your conscious mind to reprogram your deep subconsciousness by supplying affirmative suggestions, such as "I have outgrown the need to fear dark places." This is the one time affirmations can be effective. Or use your conscious mind to synthesize powerful, vivid, positive images to counteract the fearful, negative dream images of your subconscious mind. If your recurrent dream evokes the fear of being abandoned and totally alone, for example, imagine yourself as a small baby being held by you as an adult. Comfort, stroke, and speak reassuringly to your infant self. Give him or her a safe place. If your dream evokes the fear of darkness, counteract this by imagining yourself as an unborn child warm and safe in the darkness of your mother's womb. Now see yourself as a newborn baby, still warm and safe in the dark, being comforted and protected by you as an adult. Remember, unless you repudiate the unwelcome actions and feelings of your dream by affirming the opposite, you will feel guarded and uncomfortable the whole day.

In considering your dreams, keep the following in mind:

1. Dreams are the chief way your subconscious mind maintains the status quo of your defense system.
2. Your defenses are activated as much by dreams as by incidents in your daily waking life.
3. When you begin to mature emotionally or to improve your self-image, the change threatens the status quo of your defense system, and nightmares can result. The purpose of nightmares is to hold you back to your initial fears.
4. The more threatened your defense system, the more vivid, recurrent, and remembered are your dreams.
5. To analyze a dream, identify the dream's purpose and the defense aroused.
6. To understand a particular action in your dream and its implications, ignore names, gender, and places. Look only at the action and its emotional effect on you.

## SUMMARY

Your only deterrent to emotional maturity are the **emotional defenses** or **personality arrests** you form in the first six years of life. To change your behavior, you need to give up all attempts to control. **Spontaneous age reenactment** is living, everyday proof that you are trapped at an infantile or childish level of **emotional development**, but it is also the window through which the therapist trained in **directed age reenactment** can see your path to healing. By understanding and applying the dynamics of age reenactment—both spontaneous and directed—such a therapist can help you overcome unwanted and unneeded defenses.

Once you understand the origin and function of your defenses, you can prepare yourself for change. Relaxing and temporarily suspending your critical judgment will allow you to gain direct access to your **subconscious mind**, where all your defenses are formed and stored.

Through a number of basic techniques and exercises, you can learn to relax and center yourself, offset drains on your emotional energy, harness your intuitive powers, monitor your emotional defenses, and upgrade your own and your children's **self-image**. Together with directed age reenactment, these skills will help you resume—and accelerate—your stalled emotional development.

Dreams are the expression of your subconscious mind and are essential to maintain and reinforce your self-image and defense system; dream analysis is more helpful when approached from this perspective. By formulating positive affirmations and by synthesizing powerful, vivid, positive **images**, you can use your **conscious mind** to counteract the fearful, negative dream images of your subconscious mind.

# Conclusion

For countless generations we have known we cannot survive as isolated individuals but must live in social groups. Strong, sound relationships are thus of the utmost importance to prevent disharmony between individuals and war between nations or groups. Fear and anger are the two chief forces each of us learns that keep us apart.

When you observe developing infants or children, you soon find out that we don't come into this world with inborn fears and anger—we *learn* these from our parents and from society. In order to release their hold on us—and to avoid teaching them to our children—we need to understand how fear and anger are learned.

In medicine the greatest advances made to improve everyday life have been public health measures such as sanitation and inoculation, which have prevented widespread physical disease and suffering by eliminating their causes beforehand. The challenge facing us today is to prevent widespread *emotional* disease and suffering by eliminating *its* causes—fear and anger learned as infants or children.

My fondest hope is to teach all young people, parents, and grandparents that a positive, open, and loving attitude and relationship toward our children is the greatest gift we can give them. If we start right now, I believe that in four or five generations we will see a vast improvement, as fear, anger, and the tensions and conflicts they give rise to are reduced throughout the world.

Each of us has the choice.

We can pass our crippling fears and anger—our hang-ups, our emotional defenses, our personality arrests—on to our children, just as our parents passed them on to us.

Or, by releasing our fear and anger, we can provide our children, grandchildren, and future generations the chance to develop a strong, independent self-image—the chance to become everything they were born to be.

# APPENDIX

# Directed Age Reenactment

NOTE: *Directed age reenactment is* not *a do-it-yourself technique but a powerful therapeutic tool for use by trained professionals; the following explanation is in no way intended to suggest otherwise.*

Each of us every day of our lives goes into periods of spontaneous age reenactment. This reliving of past experiences happens every time we respond automatically or behave in a manner not appropriate to a current situation; our response belongs to a former time or place.

Suppose you are reading a novel in which the story line has the hero stranded on a ledge in a remote mountain site, as night is falling and a storm closing in. The vivid description causes you to react—the back of your neck gets tight, you hold your breath, your hands get sweaty, you want to get away. If you had no memory of desertion, darkness, threatening storms, or being stranded, you could not even imagine the hero's feelings in such a situation. You would have no reaction whatsoever. It is not likely that you were ever in the precise predicament described in the story, but the key elements—alone, stranded, high ledge, night falling, storm approaching—any one or all of these can stir the memory bank in your subconscious mind and cause a defensive reaction.

As you are sitting comfortably by the fire, at home, you logically need no defense reactions—breath holding, chills, sweating, stiff neck, and the like—but these come on automatically. They are a reenactment from your past—a *spontaneous* age reenactment.

In the course of developing directed age reenactment, I learned how, by carefully monitoring patients' defense reactions, to guide them safely back through the archives of their subconscious mind to the time they first felt threatened and first created a particular defense reaction within themselves—and to help them explore the circumstances (initial sensitizing event) that caused it to be fixed in their memory bank. This is possible because the subconscious mind forgets nothing; only the conscious mind forgets. The initial sensitizing event will always have taken place in the first six years of life. In many instances, patients can go directly to the event, but more likely they will go backwards stepwise in time, through a complete file of similar reactions.

The technique of directed age reenactment is straightforward and makes no use of special hypnotic induction such as imagining pages of the calendar being torn off, deep breathing, or counting backwards. The technique is most effective with persons who have few rigid character traits because they still retain unguarded their natural inquisitiveness and imagination. It also works with very controlled, rigid persons who unconsciously resist everything by their own questioning, due to their learned fearfulness, but in these cases it takes much more skill and patience on the part of the therapist.

Directed age reenactment is enhanced by the attendance of five, six, or more people, provided they also want to experience similar reactions within themselves. To a greater or lesser degree, these peripheral participants will identify with and experience the emotions relived by the patient.

A typical directed age reenactment, such as I might conduct with a male patient, for example, proceeds as follows. I sit in a chair facing the patient, a chair of equal height. I place one hand on the back of the patient's shoulder or neck and hold the patient's two hands in my second hand. I let my knees rest against the patient's knees. I gently rock the patient in an arrhythmic pattern, which helps the patient disassociate from his immediate surroundings. Then I suggest that the patient close his eyes and ask him to state the first thought that pops into his mind, no matter how inappropriate it may seem.

In this setting, I am in a position to detect the patient's slightest expression of body language, such as tension in the knees, withdrawing of the back, change in breathing, facial expression, tightness of neck muscles, hand sweating, odor of nervousness, restlessness of the feet, and any hesitant, awkward speech, voice inflection, or misplaced modifiers. In a sense, I act as a polygraph detector, but one with many more channels than the standard inanimate machine. As the peripheral participants tune into the patient, they react and, by projecting their feelings of support, strengthen the emotional aura surrounding the patient.

At the outset, I inform the patient that I really don't need to know anything about his past. In a sense I am only a conduit for what I hear, which I store in my short-term memory, which will quickly fade. In actual practice, all that is needed to start the process is to detect any body language or voice reaction—or any hesitancy in the patient's response—and to call these reactions to his attention. When I do so, he will instantly react by intensifying and heightening his emotional content (just as we blush more deeply if someone calls attention to our blushing), which will aid in identifying and tracing the source of his reaction.

If the patient is hesitant in his response and starts to draw away, tensing his back muscles, this reaction belongs properly to another time and place; it has nothing to do with the therapist or the present moment. I will ask such questions as "Who (or what situation) are you drawing away from?" "What are your feelings right now?" "Who are you with now?" "Where do you feel yourself to be?" "How old are you now?" In general I try to ask questions that are open-ended. Because the subconscious mind knows only one state of being, the present, I ask each question only in the present tense.

Being completely familiar with the Smith Index (see pages 24–25) and thoroughly experienced in identifying body language, I can age-date each manifestation of the patient's body language. If the patient's feet show an inclination to move or run, I know we are at a two-year-old level (running away). I can ask the patient directly, "As a two-year-old, who do you see yourself running away from? What situation are you running away from?" If the patient doesn't immediately respond, either verbally or physically, my question wasn't relevant, so I change the direction of the inquiry, moving on until I do get an emotional response. Then I again call the patient's reaction to his attention to intensify that reaction and proceed until I can identify the circumstances of its origin.

If the patient is **behaving as** an infant, I may ask, "Where do you see yourself now? Are you standing? What are you wearing? What time is it, day or night? Are you alone? Describe your crib, the room, the color of curtains (and so forth). Who do you feel is holding you? What does the touch of your mother feel like? Is your father in this picture? What do you hear him saying? What is the feeling you are getting from your father?"

The real purpose of directed age reenactment is for patients to return to where their emotional reactions first started (initial sensitizing event) and to understand why it was necessary for them to develop these reactions as a means of defense (survival). Once they recall this event with all its emotional content, once they become *consciously* aware of it, they will never again lose this conscious awareness.

The subconscious mind forgets nothing. The event that is inscribed the deepest is the one with greatest emotional content. When I conduct a directed age reenactment, I create a safe place for patients to feel free to relive an incident of their early life. During age reenactment, patients can safely reexperience a family conflict of great stress, complete with innumerable details. The whole family scene can be reconstructed. When patients review all this information and they add the ten, thirty, fifty, or more years' experience they have later gained, they are able to understand much more fully their initial responses, to revise their perceptions of their family relationships, and to understand their place and importance within their family group.

When working with guarded patients, I pay especial attention to their heightened fears of interpersonal involvement. When I ask a guarded female patient, for example, to tell me what first pops into her head, her answer is, "Nothing does." Because the mind cannot be without thoughts, even for an instant, if this continues it indicates a spontaneous age reenactment in itself and tells me that this patient is very fearful of divulging anything about herself. When the feeling of fear comes on strongly, the patient's whole back may become covered with sweat in two to three seconds. Secretiveness is a trait of a child four or five years old; children under four years old tend to be unguarded and effusive. Consequently, the patient's defenses are mostly going to be those of saying or doing nothing, except for the "right thing," if she can figure it out.

Even with guarded patients, there will be flashes of early emotions that inevitably break through. These will only be evident for brief moments because such patients will tend to withdraw every time they feel exposed. Nevertheless, when these fragments of reenacted memories are put in sharp focus, I am able to guide these patients in and out of reenactment and piece together a developmental pattern.

One unique feature of directed age reenactment is that patients are truly in two time frames at once. They are never out of the present nor do they lose any of their adult awareness skills or analytical ability, and at the same time because they feel safe, they are able emotionally to relive their past experiences.

When patients reenact the initial sensitizing event behind a particular defense, usually toward the end of a twenty-

or thirty-minute session, I have them review their recalled past in all its aspects, using all their present awareness. The chief objective is for patients to reexperience the full emotions of the event, which will allow them to understand that their response was the *only* logical response they had available to protect themselves at that time in their past. Therapeutically, reviewing the objective circumstances of the event is helpful, but only when patients reexperience all the emotions they first felt and apply all the learning they have acquired since that time can their perceptions change and their fear or anger be released. Only then can their emotional growth resume.

# Glossary

**acceptance.** Accepting someone for who that person *is*, without requiring him or her to *do* anything or to change in any way; a fundamental human **need**; opposed to *approval*, which demands that someone be, do, or change as the approver wishes.

**act like**. Verb phrase used to describe what you *consciously* choose to do or pretend to be, the way you act in *absence* of stress, based on how you *want* others to perceive you and what you *want* yourself to be (your **self-portrait**); opposed to "**behave as**," which describes your *actual* behavior and level of **emotional development**, the way you act when under stress, based on how you *feel* (*know*) yourself to be *subconsciously* (your **self-image**). See also **self-portrait**, **self-image**.

**active imagery**. See **imagination**.

**anger**. Along with **fear**, one of your most primitive, powerful drives for self-protection. When used only for truly life-threatening situations and then only for the briefest time necessary, **anger** can save your life at little or no cost to your body; when it is the least bit sustained, **anger** drains your body's energy. Explosive **anger** (rage) is designed to keep newborns alive at the instant they perceive a threat. Infantile uncontrolled **anger**, when repeated, prolonged, and reinforced, gives rise to the **emotional defense** (**personality arrest**) of violent temper (birth to age one), which expresses itself in later years as ranting or temper tantrums; vandalism, juvenile delinquency, wife and child beating, or other violent criminal behavior. Low-grade **anger** of infants and children (crankiness, fussiness, sullenness), when repeated, prolonged, and reinforced, gives rise to the **emotional defenses** of irritability (birth to age one); defiance or habitual profanity (age two to two and a half); aggressiveness or **passive aggressiveness** (age two and a half to three); sarcasm or bitterness and resentment (age three). See also **fear**, **emotional defense**.

**anorexia nervosa**. Extreme manifestation of the childish **personality arrest** of perfectionism formed between the ages of three and four, characterized by aversion to food, morbid fear of being overweight, and compulsive fasting. Typically affecting women in their teens and early twenties, anorexia results in excessive weight loss and malnutrition and may, unless properly treated, lead to death by starvation. Anorexics fast in a futile attempt to make their overweight **self-image** conform to their slender, "perfect" ideal. Emotionally, they are nice little girls (or, rarely, boys) whose neat, uniform penmanship reflects their constant striving for perfection and their need to control all risk in their lives. If you are anorexic, you **behave as** a rejected three-year-old desperately trying to make yourself "right" by compulsively fasting—but always *feeling* yourself to be fat, no matter how thin you become.

**awareness**. Being in touch with something using whatever senses you need—sight, hearing, taste, smell, touch, **intuition**; perceiving something as it really *is*; the opposite of **fear**, control, and **emotional defenses**, which block **awareness**. Your ability to deal with change—and therefore with life itself—is directly proportional to your **awareness**, which automatically increases each time you relax. Common sense amounts to **awareness** of your surroundings; when you are fully aware of all the information available in any given situation, you seldom make foolish decisions. As your **awareness** increases, your openness affords you more options and you realize that nature and the world around you are ever more supporting.

**behave as**. Verb phrase used to describe your *actual* behavior and level of **emotional development**, the way you act when under stress, based on how you *feel* (*know*) yourself to be *subconsciously* (your **self-image**); opposed to "**act like**," which describes what you *consciously* choose to do or pretend to be, the way you act in *absence* of stress, based on how you *want* others to perceive you and what you *want* yourself to be (your **self-portrait**). See also **self-image, self-portrait**.

**childhood**. Period in your life from two and a half to six years of age, when you are establishing and adjusting to your life as a member of your family or group; by the age of six, your **self-image** is all but fully set. Because children can see it is to their benefit to change, where infants cannot, the **personality arrests** formed in **childhood** are usually easier to overcome than those formed in **infancy**. See also **infancy**.

**claustrophobia**. Severe manifestation of the infantile **personality arrest** of withdrawal formed *before birth*, characterized by morbid fear of enclosed or confined spaces. As a claustrophobe, whenever you feel threatened by close physical circumstances—low ceilings, small rooms, narrow corridors—that remind your subconscious of what you faced in the womb, you frantically seek escape from confinement.

**compound personality arrest**. Combination—in response to repeated and prolonged emotional threats—of two or more **personality arrests (emotional defenses)**, acting cumulatively, in concert; for example, when combined, poor body image (age one) and performance anxiety (age four) become the **compound personality arrest** of chronic impotence (age four); the three-year-old defenses of bitterness and resentment and blind obedience become the **compound personality arrest** of bigotry (age five); and the five-year-old defenses of hatred —itself a **converted personality arrest**—and dogmatism become the **compound personality arrest** of vengefulness (age five). See also **converted personality arrest**.

**conscious mind**. Part of your mind that allows you to control your voluntary (skeletal) muscles, combine and rearrange **images**, analyze, apply logic, and make comparisons, decisions, criticisms, and judgments. Your **conscious mind** tells you what you *think*—or *want*—yourself to be (your **self-portrait**). See also **subconscious mind**.

**converted personality arrest**. Conversion—in response to repeated and prolonged emotional threats—of a **personality arrest** (**emotional defense**) generally formed at an earlier age; for example, violent temper (birth to age one) becomes the **converted personality arrest** of hatred (age five). See also **compound personality arrest**.

**depression**. Childish **personality arrest** formed between the ages of two and a half and three, characterized by emotional dejection deeper and more prolonged than warranted by any objective reason. **Depression** comes and goes, lasting for quite a while or for a relatively short time. Depressed people are nearly always sad, gloomy, or listless and cannot explain why they feel the way they do; often their movements are slow, their concentration poor, and they have difficulty thinking or eating normally; their usual self-reliance is replaced by feelings of despair and uselessness. If as an adult you are depressed, more than likely at two and a half you urgently needed your parents' **acceptance** but were faced instead with their disapproval or rejection. You felt trapped and protected yourself by becoming depressed, by shutting down your feelings, your expression, your activity—everything that might further displease your parents.

**directed age reenactment**. Therapeutic technique designed to help patients understand, come to grips with, and release their **emotional defenses** (**personality arrests**) by *consciously* invoking the circumstances (**initial sensitizing events**) that led to the formation of those defenses in their infancy or early childhood; the process itself. In **directed age reenactment** therapists create an emotionally safe or protected environment, gently guiding patients back to the age appropriate to a given **emotional defense** and following the path of their patients' increasing emotional intensity to the

**initial sensitizing event** itself; patients maintain their adult perspective as they recall and reexamine details of the event and reexperience their feelings associated with it. See also **spontaneous age reenactment**.

**emotional defense**. Subconscious defense created out of **fear**, during the first six years of life, in response to perceived threats of rejection, abandonment, or death, your parents' fears and **anger**—or both. An **emotional defense** is automatically activated by any current situation that reminds your **subconscious mind** of when you first formed the defense (**initial sensitizing event**)—automatically, you **behave as** the infant or child you were at that time (**spontaneous age reenactment**), responding to the perceived threat as you first did by acting out or withdrawing, regardless of how self-defeating or inappropriate your behavior is in light of the current situation; commonly called "hang-up." See also **personality arrest**, **compound personality arrest**.

**emotional development**. Natural maturation and refinement of emotional reactions. In the absence of **personality arrests**, infants emotionally develop into warm, open, and loving adults.

**emotional openness**. Natural emotional growth unsuppressed by **fear** or **anger**.

**fantasy**. Process by which your **conscious mind** *synthesizes* a desired event or situation by combining *un*real (incomplete, unexperienced) **images** from your **subconscious mind**, entirely apart from what you have learned, felt, or experienced to that moment—and contrary to what you intuitively *know* to be true; the event or situation so synthesized. Based on wishful thinking, **fantasy** involves no attempt to assess the feasibility of what you fantasize. See also **imagination**.

**fault**. Painful feeling of being to blame, originally *assumed* by you for stressful events or situations beyond your control. You come to feel "at fault" because you did nothing to

You come to feel "at fault" because you did nothing to prevent or remedy these events or situations (even though you weren't the cause); like **shame**, **fault** stifles your **emotional development**. See also **shame**.

**fear**. Along with **anger**, one of your most primitive, powerful drives for self-protection and the main self-limiting factor in your life. The basic nature of **fear** is **imagination**; almost all your fears are imagined. Although vital in split-second reactions to avert sudden dangers, **fear** blocks your **awareness**, interferes with your understanding, and thus greatly impairs your ability to deal with prolonged dangers, emotional situations, and with life itself. You create some of your fears but learn most from your **parents**; as an infant or child in the first six years of your life, you respond to these fears by forming **emotional defenses** (from **depression** to rage) to save yourself from rejection, abandonment, and death. Through these defenses, your **fear** "protects" you from other people or situations (imagined threats), imprisoning you in an infantile or childish state of reaction, blocking your **emotional development**, draining your emotional energy, and thus severely limiting your life options. See also **anger**, **emotional defense**.

**guilt**. Painful feeling of being to blame, originally induced by others to punish you for *doing* something they consider wrong (or for *not* doing something they consider right); usually imposed by parents on their children as a means of emotional manipulation or control. Temporary, limited **guilt** serves to alert you to having acted in a manner *you* consider thoughtless, inconsiderate, or wrong—in time to do something about it; otherwise **guilt** only debilitates, focusing single-mindedly on the *past*, which cannot be changed. See also **responsibility**.

**hang-up**. See **emotional defense**.

**image**. Basic memory unit and the activator of your **subconscious mind**, containing all the sensory components (sight, touch, hearing, smell, taste, and **intuition**) of your original thought or experience; when incomplete, a *synthesized* product of your **conscious** and **subconscious mind**, based on wishful thinking. See also **imagination**, **fantasy**.

**imagination**. Process by which your **conscious mind** visualizes an event or situation in vivid detail by combining real **images** from your **subconscious mind** based on everything you have learned, felt, or experienced to that moment —and everything you intuitively *know* to be true—and by assessing the feasibility of what you imagine; sometimes called "active imagery." See also **fantasy**.

**infancy**. Period in your life from before birth to two and a half years of age, when you are single-handedly establishing your identity and individuality. Because infants live only in the present and therefore can't see the need for change, the **personality arrests** formed in **infancy** are more deeply rooted and usually harder to overcome than those formed later on.

**initial sensitizing event**. Circumstances that first led you to form a particular **emotional defense**, in the first six years of life, when you protected yourself from the perceived threat of rejection, abandonment, and death by acting out or withdrawing; so named by analogy with the mechanism of immune response. Your **emotional defense**, logical and understandable for an infant or child at the time of the **initial sensitizing event**, becomes self-defeating or inappropriate for an adult in circumstances that (objectively) pose little or no threat. See also **emotional defense**.

**intuition**. Seat of creative thinking in your **subconscious mind**; your inner or "sixth" sense, which (together with your five physical senses) gives you access to your ancestral understanding (**knowledge**) and which lets you *know* things that elude your **conscious mind** and your powers of logic. How you treat your **intuition** affects your **self-image** and determines your **self-esteem**—each time you trust in your

**intuition**, you strengthen your **self-image** and raise your **self-esteem**; each time you *override* your **intuition**, you weaken your **self-image** and *lower* your **self-esteem**. See also **imagination**, **subconscious mind**.

**kleptomania**. Severe manifestation of the childish **personality arrest** of perfectionism formed between the ages of three and four, characterized by a compulsion to steal. Kleptomaniacs steal on impulse, again and again, often unaware of what they are stealing—or even *that* they are stealing. If you are a kleptomaniac, you **behave as** a rejected three-year-old desperately trying to make things "right" for yourself by taking what belongs to others.

**knowledge**. Understanding inherited from your ancestors and encoded in your brain; accessible through your senses—sight, hearing, touch, taste, smell, and especially **intuition**. See also **learning**, **intuition**.

**learning**. Understanding gained through information, practice, and experience in the course of your lifetime. See also **knowledge**.

**love**. Feeling toward another person that arises automatically when you know the other accepts you for who you *are*; **love** draws on your primary drive to recognize and protect your own body (life), which you naturally extend to your children, relatives, tribe; opposed to commonly accepted modern sense of "love": active energy you put forth voluntarily or involuntarily toward another person for your own benefit or satisfaction in the hope that the other person will appreciate and return it to you according to your expectations. See also **acceptance**.

**needs**. What you in your **subconscious mind** *feel—know—* you need; for example, **acceptance** or intimacy. **Needs** fulfilled bring lasting satisfaction and create a sense that you have grown or developed, that your life has an added dimension. See also **wants.**

**parent**. Adult—whether biological, adopted, or foster parent, other relative, or guardian—principally responsible for the care and rearing of a child.

**passive aggressiveness**. Childish **personality arrest** formed between the ages of two and a half and three, arising from low-grade **anger** when repeated, prolonged, and reinforced, and characterized by passive resistance to demands of others. Passive aggressive people express their **anger** indirectly and nonviolently—by pretending to comply, by procrastinating, or by being petulant, unresponsive, constantly late, or deliberately inefficient. Also called "passive aggression."

**personality arrest**. Blocking of part of your **emotional development**, during the first six years of life, by the formation of an **emotional defense**; the part of the personality so blocked or the **emotional defense** causing the block—usually so complete that you are unable even to acknowledge, much less discuss, it.

**responsibility**. **Awareness** of the consequences of your actions based on respect for, and caring about, others and yourself; first developed between the ages of three and a half and four and a half. **Responsibility** focuses on the present and future and inclines you to choose actions that will help others, to avoid actions that will hurt them, and, where it is within your power, to correct unintended hurt or damage. See also **guilt**.

**satiety**. End of physiological hunger; part of a natural reflex and your body's signal you have eaten enough—as opposed to the feeling of *fullness*, which is your body's signal that you have grossly *over*eaten and are now storing food in your fat reserve. Most often acting out of their own anxiety, parents teach their babies to *consciously override* **satiety**, which creates in them confusion of emotional with physiological hunger, a compulsion to overeat (**emotional defense**), and a lifelong tendency to become overweight or obese.

**schizophrenia.** Extreme manifestation of the infantile **personality arrest** of withdrawal formed *before birth*, characterized by a distorted sense of reality, tendency to live in a world of private fantasy, and inability to maintain normal interpersonal relationships; psychosis whose symptoms typically include apathetic withdrawal or bizarre activity and sometimes speech disturbances, ambivalence, inappropriate or constricted emotional response, delusions, feelings of persecution, and hallucinations. As a schizophrenic, whenever you feel threatened by circumstances that remind you of what you faced in the womb, you desperately withdraw into yourself.

**self-esteem.** Feeling that you can trust and rely on yourself, that you are okay as you *are*. Your **self-esteem** is based on your **self-image** and determined by how you trust and respond to your deepest feelings—your **intuition**. Each time you trust your **intuition**, you raise your **self-esteem**; each time you *override* your **intuition**, you *lower* your **self-esteem**. See also **intuition**, **self-image**.

**self-image.** What you in your **subconscious mind** *know—feel*—you are. All but fully set by the time you are six, your **self-image** reflects your level of **emotional development** (therefore also your **personality arrests** as they affect your development) and determines your *actual* behavior—you **behave as** your **self-image**. Although you can't change your past environment, your mother, your father, your friends, your children, your spouse, or even yourself (directly), you *can* change your perceptions and consequently your expectations *and* your **self-image**. See also **self-portrait**, **behave as**.

**self-portrait.** What you in your **conscious mind** *think—want*—yourself to be. In the absence of stress, you can **act like** your **self-portrait**, often quite convincingly and for some time, but as soon as you are under stress, you immediately **behave as** your **self-image**, reverting to the infant or child you were when your **emotional development** was arrested. See also **self-image**, **act like**.

**shame**. Painful feeling of inadequacy, originally induced by others to punish you for *being* someone they consider inferior (or for *not* being someone they consider superior); **shame** may also make you feel that you are carrying the heavy burden of your family's secrets. Like **guilt**, only more destructive and always debilitating, **shame** is usually imposed by parents on their children as a means of emotional manipulation or control. See also **guilt**.

**sixth sense**. See **intuition**.

**spontaneous age reenactment.** Automatic behavioral reaction invoked by your **subconscious mind** as part of an **emotional defense**. In response to a current situation that reminds your **subconscious mind** of when you first formed your **emotional defense** (**initial sensitizing event**), you **behave as** the infant or child you were *then*, acting out against or withdrawing from the threat you perceived at that time. Others typically react to your **spontaneous age reenactment** by telling you, "You're acting like a baby (child)!" See also **directed age reenactment**, **emotional defense**.

**subconscious mind**. Part of your mind that automatically controls (through your autonomic nervous system) ninety percent of your bodily processes, including your physical senses (sight, hearing, smell, touch, and taste), your immune system, and your physical reflexes; that stores memories (as **images**) of everything you have learned, felt, or experienced; that activates your **emotional defenses** and reactions; and that allows you to think creatively or intuitively, using your **intuition** or "sixth sense." Your **subconscious mind**, which tells you what you *know*—or *feel*—yourself to be (your **self-image**), gives you access (through your **intuition**) to understanding inherited from your ancestors (**knowledge**) and to the common consciousness, or universal mind, of humanity. See also **conscious mind**.

**unworthiness**. Infantile **personality arrest** formed between the ages of two and two and a half, characterized by low

**self-esteem** and by socially obnoxious, self-destructive behavior; often expressed as alcoholism, compulsive gambling, and rowdiness. See also **worthlessness**.

**wants**. What you in your **conscious mind** *think* you need; for example, a new car or a special person for a partner. **Wants** fulfilled may bring you momentary satisfaction, but—in and of themselves—they don't create any lasting or convincing feeling that you have grown or developed, or that you have enlarged your **awareness** of the world you live in. See also **needs**.

**wisdom.** Deeper understanding of the world acquired by combining **learning** with **knowledge**. See also **learning**, **knowledge**.

**worthlessness**. Infantile **personality arrest** formed before the age of one, characterized by extremely low **self-esteem** and by *criminal disregard* for others or self; more destructive and more deeply rooted than **unworthiness**; often expressed as addiction to hard or mind-altering drugs, extreme alcoholism (to or past the point of physical and mental breakdown), drunk driving, and wife or child beating. See also **unworthiness**.